T0343874

CAMBRIDGE
UNIVERSITY PRESS

Combined and Co-ordinated Sciences

for Cambridge IGCSE™

BIOLOGY WORKBOOK

David Martindill, Michael Smyth, Mary Jones & Geoff Jones

CAMBRIDGE
UNIVERSITY PRESS

Shaftesbury Road, Cambridge CB2 8EA, United Kingdom

One Liberty Plaza, 20th Floor, New York, NY 10006, USA

477 Williamstown Road, Port Melbourne, VIC 3207, Australia

314–321, 3rd Floor, Plot 3, Splendor Forum, Jasola District Centre, New Delhi – 110025, India

103 Penang Road, #05–06/07, Visioncrest Commercial, Singapore 238467

Cambridge University Press is part of the University of Cambridge.

It furthers the University's mission by disseminating knowledge in the pursuit of education, learning and research at the highest international levels of excellence.

www.cambridge.org
Information on this title: www.cambridge.org/9781009311304

First published 2017
Second edition 2023

20 19 18 17 16 15 14 13 12 11 10 9 8 7 6

Printed in Poland by Opolgraf

A catalogue record for this publication is available from the British Library

ISBN 978-1-009-31130-4 Workbook with Digital Access

Additional resources for this publication at www.cambridge.org/9781009311304

Cambridge University Press has no responsibility for the persistence or accuracy of URLs for external or third-party internet websites referred to in this publication, and does not guarantee that any content on such websites is, or will remain, accurate or appropriate. Information regarding prices, travel timetables, and other factual information given in this work is correct at the time of first printing but Cambridge University Press does not guarantee the accuracy of such information thereafter.

....

NOTICE TO TEACHERS IN THE UK
It is illegal to reproduce any part of this work in material form (including photocopying and electronic storage) except under the following circumstances:
(i)   where you are abiding by a licence granted to your school or institution by the Copyright Licensing Agency;
(ii) where no such licence exists, or where you wish to exceed the terms of a licence, and you have gained the written permission of Cambridge University Press;
(iii) where you are allowed to reproduce without permission under the provisions of Chapter 3 of the Copyright, Designs and Patents Act 1988, which covers, for example, the reproduction of short passages within certain types of educational anthology and reproduction for the purposes of setting examination questions.

....

Endorsement statement

Endorsement indicates that a resource has passed Cambridge International's rigorous quality-assurance process and is suitable to support the delivery of a Cambridge International syllabus. However, endorsed resources are not the only suitable materials available to support teaching and learning, and are not essential to be used to achieve the qualification. Resource lists found on the Cambridge International website will include this resource and other endorsed resources.

Any example answers to questions taken from past question papers, practice questions, accompanying marks and mark schemes included in this resource have been written by the authors and are for guidance only. They do not replicate examination papers. In examinations the way marks are awarded may be different. Any references to assessment and/or assessment preparation are the publisher's interpretation of the syllabus requirements. Examiners will not use endorsed resources as a source of material for any assessment set by Cambridge International.

While the publishers have made every attempt to ensure that advice on the qualification and its assessment is accurate, the official syllabus, specimen assessment materials and any associated assessment guidance materials produced by the awarding body are the only authoritative source of information and should always be referred to for definitive guidance. Cambridge International recommends that teachers consider using a range of teaching and learning resources based on their own professional judgement of their students' needs.

Cambridge International has not paid for the production of this resource, nor does Cambridge International receive any royalties from its sale. For more information about the endorsement process, please visit www.cambridgeinternational.org/endorsed-resources

Cambridge International copyright material in this publication is reproduced under licence and remains the intellectual property of Cambridge Assessment International Education.

Third party websites and resources referred to in this publication have not been endorsed by Cambridge Assessment International Education.

CAMBRIDGE DEDICATED TEACHER AWARDS

2022

Teachers play an important part in shaping futures. Our Dedicated Teacher Awards recognise the hard work that teachers put in every day.

Thank you to everyone who nominated this year; we have been inspired and moved by all of your stories. Well done to all of our nominees for your dedication to learning and for inspiring the next generation of thinkers, leaders and innovators.

Congratulations to our incredible winners!

WINNER

Regional Winner Australia, New Zealand & South-East Asia	Regional Winner Europe	Regional Winner North & South America	Regional Winner Central & Southern Africa	Regional Winner Middle East & North Africa	Regional Winner East & South Asia
Mohd Al Khalifa Bin Mohd Affnan Keningau Vocational College, Malaysia	Dr. Mary Shiny Ponparambil Paul Little Flower English School, Italy	Noemi Falcon Zora Neale Hurston Elementary School, United States	Temitope Adewuyi Fountain Heights Secondary School, Nigeria	Uroosa Imran Beaconhouse School System KG-1 branch, Pakistan	Jeenath Akther Chittagong Grammar School, Bangladesh

For more information about our dedicated teachers and their stories, go to
dedicatedteacher.cambridge.org

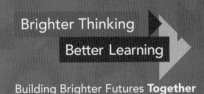

Brighter Thinking
Better Learning
Building Brighter Futures **Together**

› Contents

> How to use this series

We offer a comprehensive, flexible array of resources for the Cambridge IGCSE™ Combined and Co-ordinated Sciences syllabuses. We provide targeted support and practice for the specific challenges we've heard that students face: learning science with English as a second language; structured learning for all; and developing practical skills.

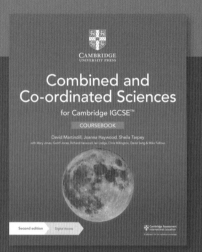

The coursebook provides coverage of the full Cambridge IGCSE™ Combined and Co-ordinated syllabuses. Each chapter explains facts and concepts, and uses relevant real-world examples of scientific principles to bring the subject to life. Together with a focus on practical work and plenty of active learning opportunities, the coursebook prepares learners for all aspects of their scientific study. Questions and practice questions in every chapter help learners to consolidate their understanding and provide practice opportunities to apply their learning.

The teacher's resource contains detailed guidance for all topics of the syllabuses, including common misconceptions identifying areas where learners might need extra support, as well as an engaging bank of lesson ideas for each syllabus topic. Differentiation is emphasised with advice for identification of different learner needs and suggestions of appropriate interventions to support and stretch learners. The teacher's resource also contains support for preparing and carrying out all the investigations in the practical workbook, including a set of sample results for when practicals aren't possible.

The teacher's resource also contains scaffolded worksheets and unit tests for each chapter. Answers for all components are accessible to teachers for free on the Cambridge Go platform.

The skills-focused workbooks have been carefully constructed to help learners develop the skills that they need as they progress through their Cambridge IGCSE™ Combined and Co-ordinated Sciences course, providing further practice of some of the topics in the coursebook, each science with its own separate workbook. A three-tier, scaffolded approach to skills development enables students to gradually progress through 'focus', 'practice' and 'challenge' exercises, ensuring that every learner is supported. The workbooks enable independent learning and are ideal for use in class or as homework.

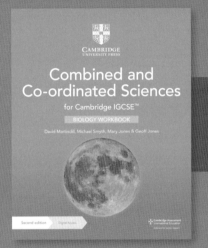

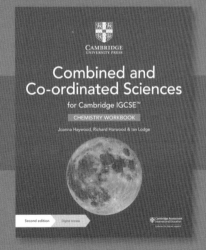

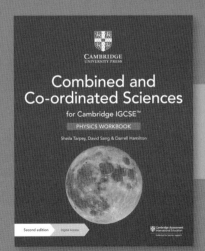

> How to use this book

Throughout this book, you will notice lots of different features that will help your learning. These are explained below.

LEARNING INTENTIONS

These set the scene for each exercise and indicate the important concepts.

KEY WORDS

Definitions for useful vocabulary are given at the start of each section. You will also find definitions for these words in the Glossary at the back of this book.

TIP

The information in these boxes will help you complete the exercises, and give you support in areas that you might find difficult.

Exercises

These help you to practise skills that are important for studying Cambridge IGCSE Biology.

Questions within exercises fall into one of three types:

- Focus questions will help build your basic skills.

- Practice questions provide more opportunities for practice, pushing your skills further.

- Challenge questions will stretch and challenge you even further.

SELF/PEER ASSESSMENT

At the end of some exercises, you will find opportunities to help you assess your own work, or that of your classmates, and consider how you can improve the way you learn.

〉 Introduction

This workbook covers two syllabuses: Cambridge IGCSE Combined Science (0653) and Cambridge IGCSE and IGCSE (9-1) Co-ordinated Sciences syllabuses (0654/0973). Before you start using this workbook, check with your teacher which syllabus you are studying and which papers you will take. You will sit either the Core paper or the Extended paper for your syllabus. If you are sitting the Extended paper, you will study the Core material and the Supplement material for your syllabus.

Once you know which paper you will be sitting, you can use the exercises in this workbook to help develop the skills you need and prepare for your examination.

The examination tests three different Assessment Objectives, or AOs for short. These are:

AO1 Knowledge with understanding

AO2 Handling information and problem solving

AO3 Experimental skills and investigations.

Just learning your work and remembering it (AO1) is not enough to make sure that you achieve your best result in your exam. You also need to be able to use what you've learned in unfamiliar contexts (AO2) and to demonstrate your experimental skills (AO3).

There are lots of activities in your coursebook which will help you to develop your experimental skills by doing practical work. This workbook contains exercises to help you to develop AO2 and AO3 further. There are some questions that just involve remembering things you have been taught (AO1), but most of the questions require you to use what you've learned to work out, for example, what a set of data means, or to suggest how an experiment might be improved.

These exercises are not intended to be exactly like the questions you would get in your exam papers. This is because they are meant to help you to develop your skills, rather than testing you on them.

There's an introduction at the start of each exercise that tells you the purpose of it, and which skills you will be working with as you answer the questions.

There are sidebars in the margins of the book to show which material relates to each syllabus and paper. If there is no sidebar, it means that everyone will study this material.

Use this table to ensure that you study the right material for your syllabus and paper:

Cambridge IGCSE Combined Science (0653)		Cambridge IGCSE Co-ordinated Sciences (0654)	
Core	Supplement	Core	Supplement
You will study the material:	You will study the material:	You will study the material:	You will study everything, which includes the material:
Without a sidebar	Without a sidebar	Without a sidebar	Without a sidebar
	With a dashed grey sidebar	With a solid grey sidebar	With a dashed grey sidebar
	With a dashed black sidebar	With a dashed black sidebar	With a dashed black sidebar
			With a solid grey sidebar
	You will _not_ study material with a solid grey sidebar or a solid black sidebar.	You will _not_ study material with a solid black sidebar or a dashed grey sidebar.	With a solid black sidebar

A simplified table has also been included on the inside back flap of this workbook to open out and view alongside the exercises.

Safety

A few practical exercises have been included. These could be carried out at home using simple materials that you are likely to have available to you.

While carrying out such experiments, it is your responsibility to think about your own safety, and the safety of others. Work sensibly, under supervision, and assess any risks before starting. If you are in doubt, discuss what you are going to do with your teacher before you start.

Cells and organisms

> Characteristics of living organisms

Exercise 1.1

IN THIS EXERCISE YOU WILL:

- practise naming and describing the characteristics of living things.

Focus

1   Draw lines to match each term with its description.

Term	Description
nutrition	making more of the same kind of organism
respiration	removing waste products of metabolism
growth	a permanent increase in size and dry mass
excretion	taking in materials for energy, growth and development
reproduction	chemical reactions that release energy from nutrient molecules

KEY WORDS

excretion: the removal of waste products of metabolism and substances in excess of requirements.

growth: a permanent increase in size and dry mass.

metabolic reactions: chemical reactions that take place in living organisms.

movement: an action by an organism or part of an organism causing a change of position or place.

nutrition: the taking in of materials for energy, growth and development.

organism: a living thing.

reproduction: the processes that make more of the same kind of organism.

respiration: the chemical reactions in cells that break down nutrient molecules and release energy for metabolism.

Practice

2   Figure 1.1 shows a plant, growing towards the light. Inside its leaves, photosynthesis is taking place. Photosynthesis uses carbon dioxide to make glucose, and releases oxygen.

Add labels to Figure 1.1. Your labels should include short descriptions stating how the plant is showing these characteristics of living things:

- reproduction
- growth
- sensitivity
- excretion.

KEY WORD

sensitivity: the ability to detect and respond to changes in the internal or external environment.

Figure 1.1: A plant growing towards the light.

Challenge

3   Imagine that someone from another planet is visiting Earth. They see aeroplanes and birds moving through the sky.

Explain to the visitor why birds are alive and aeroplanes are not alive, even though they seem to share some of the characteristics of living things.

....

....

....

....

....

....

› Cell structure
Exercise 1.2

IN THIS EXERCISE YOU WILL:

- practise drawing and labelling animal and plant cells
- outline the functions of some of the parts of cells
- use information to explain some of the features of a specialised cell.

Focus

Figure 1.2 shows an animal cell and the outline of a plant cell.

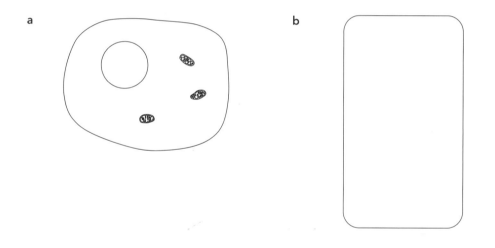

Figure 1.2 a: An animal cell. **b:** A plant cell.

1   On the animal cell diagram, label these parts:

   cell membrane   cytoplasm   mitochondrion   nucleus

2   Complete the diagram of the plant cell, and then label these parts:

   cell membrane   cell wall   chloroplast

   vacuole containing cell sap   cytoplasm   mitochondrion

   nucleus   membrane around vacuole

KEY WORDS

aerobic respiration: a chemical reaction that happens in mitochondria, where oxygen is used to release energy from glucose.

bacteria: unicellular organisms whose cells do not contain a nucleus.

cell: the smallest unit from which all organisms are made.

cell membrane: a very thin layer surrounding the cytoplasm of every cell; it controls what enters and leaves the cell.

cell sap: the fluid that fills the large vacuoles in plant cells.

cell wall: a tough layer outside the cell membrane; found in the cells of plants, fungi and bacteria.

cellulose: a carbohydrate that forms long fibres, and makes up the cell walls of plants.

chromosome: a length of DNA, found in the nucleus of a cell; it contains genetic information in the form of many different genes.

cytoplasm: the jelly-like material that fills a cell.

SELF ASSESSMENT

How confident do you feel about drawing a plant cell? Give yourself a mark for each of the points in the checklist. Award yourself:

2 marks if you did it well

1 mark if you made a good attempt at it and partly succeeded

0 marks if you did not try to do it, or did not succeed

Checklist	Marks awarded
I used a sharp pencil for drawing.	
I drew single, clean lines; the lines are not broken or fuzzy.	
I did not use any shading or colours.	
I drew the parts of the cell in the right place.	
I drew label lines with a ruler.	
Each label line touches the part it is labelling.	
Total (out of 12):	

Practice

3 a Describe the function of each of these parts in a plant cell.

Cell membrane

....

....

Mitochondrion

....

....

KEY WORDS

DNA: a molecule that contains genetic information, in the form of genes, that controls the proteins that are made in the cell.

fully permeable: allows all molecules and ions to pass through it.

Chloroplast

....

....

b When a plant is growing, new cells are produced. Describe where these new cells come from.

....

....

4 Describe the function of each of these parts in a bacterial cell.

Cell wall

....

....

Ribosome

....

....

Circular DNA

....

....

KEY WORDS

mitochondrion: a small structure in a cell, where aerobic respiration releases energy from glucose.

nucleus: a structure containing DNA in the form of chromosomes.

partially permeable: allows some molecules and ions to pass through, but not others.

ribosomes: very small structures in a cell that use information in DNA to make protein molecules.

vacuole: a fluid-filled space inside a cell, separated from the cytoplasm by a membrane.

5 Arrange these four terms in order from smallest and simplest to largest and most complex.

organ   tissue   organ system   cell

Challenge

6   Neurones are cells that transmit electrical signals throughout the body.
    This requires a lot of energy. They also synthesise (make) proteins, which help
    them to communicate with other neurones nearby.

    Use this information to explain why neurones contain many mitochondria and
    many ribosomes.

    ....

    ....

    ....

    ....

    ....

> Specialised cells and sizes of specimens

Exercise 1.3

IN THIS EXERCISE YOU WILL:

- use the magnification equation

- practise giving answers to a required number of decimal places

- practise rearranging the magnification equation

- convert from millimetres to micrometres (μm) when using the magnification equation.

KEY WORD
magnification: how many times larger an image is than the actual object.

Focus

1   Complete the equation that we can use to calculate magnification.

    magnification = ————————————

2   An apple is 60 mm in diameter. In a photograph of the apple, the apple is 120 mm in diameter. What is the magnification of the photograph? Show your working.

....

3   Figure 1.3 shows a leaf.

Figure 1.3: A leaf.

The actual length of the leaf (including the stalk) is 32 mm.

a   Measure the length of the leaf in Figure 1.3. Write down your answer.

....

b   Calculate the magnification of the leaf image in Figure 1.3. Show your working. Give your answer to one decimal place.

....

Practice

4 Look at the drawing of an animal shown in Figure 1.4.

Figure 1.4: A chameleon.

a Measure the length of the animal from its nose to the base of its tail.

....

b The actual length of this animal is 105 mm.

Calculate the magnification of the diagram.

Show your working and give your answer to *two* decimal places.

TIP
If an object is drawn smaller than its actual size, then the magnification is less than 1.

....

5 A photograph of an ant shows the length of the ant's antennae to be 25 mm. The magnification of the photograph is ×12.

Calculate the actual size of the ant's antennae. Show your working and give your answer in millimetres, to the nearest whole number.

....

Challenge

6   Figure 1.5 shows a specialised cell.

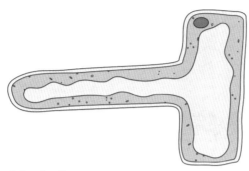

Figure 1.5: A specialised cell.

a   Name this cell *and* describe its function.

....

....

....

b   An actual root hair cell is about 100 μm long.

Calculate the magnification of the diagram. Show your working.
Give your answer to *three* significant figures.

....

Chapter 2

Movement into and out of cells

> Diffusion

Exercise 2.1

IN THIS EXERCISE YOU WILL:

- calculate means, to complete a results chart

- decide whether a set of results supports a hypothesis

- think about the design of an experiment, including standardising variables

- think about factors that affect the rate of diffusion

- identify sources of error and suggest improvements.

KEY WORDS

concentration gradient: an imaginary 'slope' from a high concentration to a low concentration.

dependent variable: the variable that you measure, as you collect your results.

diffusion: the net movement of particles from a region of their higher concentration to a region of their lower concentration (i.e. down a concentration gradient), as a result of their random movement.

independent variable: the variable that you change in an experiment.

net movement: overall or average movement.

A learner did an experiment to test this hypothesis:

The higher the temperature, the faster diffusion takes place.

She took four Petri dishes containing agar jelly. She cut four holes in the jelly in each dish, as shown in Figure 2.1.

She placed $0.5\,cm^3$ of a solution containing a red dye (coloured substance) into each hole.

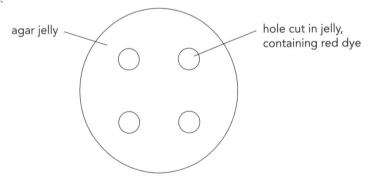

agar jelly

hole cut in jelly, containing red dye

Figure 2.1: Petri dish of agar jelly with four holes.

The learner then covered the dishes and carefully placed them in incubators set at different temperatures.

She left them for two hours. Then she measured how far the red dye had moved into the agar around each hole.

Table 2.1 shows the learner's results.

Dish	Temperature/°C	Distance red dye had moved into the jelly/mm				
		Hole 1	Hole 2	Hole 3	Hole 4	Mean (average)
A	10	2	3	2	3	
B	20	5	5	6	4	
C	40	9	11	8	10	
D	80	19	21	18	22	

Table 2.1

> **KEY WORD**
>
> **particles:** (in this context) the smallest pieces of which a substance is made; particles can be molecules, atoms or ions.

Focus

1   a   Explain what caused the red dye to move into the jelly.

....

....

....

b   Complete Table 2.1 by calculating the mean distance moved by the red dye in each dish. Write your answers in the table.

2   Deduce whether the results support the learner's hypothesis or not. Explain your answer.

....

....

....

> **TIP**
>
> The learner measured the distances to the nearest whole millimetre. You therefore need to give the mean distances to the nearest whole millimetre as well.

Practice

3   State *four* variables that the learner kept constant, or that she should have kept constant, in the experiment.

First variable ....

Second variable ....

Third variable ....

Fourth variable ....

4   Explain why it was a good idea to have four holes in each dish, rather than only one.

....

....

5   Use your knowledge of diffusion to explain the pattern shown by the mean distances the red dye diffused at different temperatures.

....

....

....

Challenge

Sources of error are features of an experiment that reduce your trust in the results.

Sources of error do not include mistakes that the learner might make, such as measuring a distance incorrectly. They are inbuilt uncertainties because of limitations of the apparatus, or the procedure.

An important source of error in the learner's experiment is the difficulty in deciding exactly where to measure to, because there is not a sharp edge where the colour of dye stops.

6   a   Identify *one* other possible source of error in the learner's experiment that would reduce the level of trust that she has in her results.

....

....

b   Suggest how the learner could modify the experiment to reduce this source of error.

....

....

› Osmosis

Exercise 2.2

IN THIS EXERCISE YOU WILL:

- organise results and put them into a results chart

- identify anomalous results

- practise drawing a line graph

- suggest how an experiment can be improved

- describe osmosis in terms of water potential

- use specific terms for the effects of osmosis on cells.

A learner investigated the effect of different concentrations of sugar solutions on some potato cylinders.

He took a large potato and used a cork borer to cut out several cylinders, each exactly the same diameter. He removed the peel from the ends of the cylinders, and then cut them into exactly 1 cm lengths. He then measured the mass of each piece.

He placed one piece of potato in each of six beakers. He covered each piece with either water or one of five different concentrations of sugar solution. He used the same volume of solution in each beaker.

The learner left the potato pieces in the beakers for 45 minutes. Then he removed them from the beakers, blotted them dry with filter paper and measured their mass again.

These were the results he wrote down.

Before	piece A = 5.2 g	piece B = 5.1 g	piece C = 4.9 g
	piece D = 5.0 g	piece E = 5.1 g	piece F = 5.2 g
Solutions	A, distilled water	B, 0.1% sugar solution	C, 0.2% solution
	D, 0.5% solution	E, 0.8% solution	F, 1.0% solution
After	A = 5.5 g	B = 5.2 g	C = 4.9 g
	D = 5.3 g	E = 5.0 g	F = 5.0 g

KEY WORDS

compound: a substance formed by the chemical combination of two or more elements in fixed proportions.

flaccid: a description of a plant cell that is soft.

high water potential: an area where there are a lot of water molecules – a dilute solution.

low water potential: an area where there are not many water molecules – a concentrated solution.

osmosis: the diffusion of water molecules through a partially permeable membrane.

osmosis: (in terms of water potential) the net movement of water molecules from a region of higher water potential (dilute solution) to a region of lower water potential (concentrated solution) through a partially permeable membrane.

Focus

1 Complete the results in Table 2.2. The first row has been done for you.

	Percentage concentration of solution	Mass / g		
		Before soaking	After soaking	Change
A	0.0	5.2	5.5	+0.3
B				
C				
D				
E				
F				

Table 2.2

KEY WORDS

partially permeable membrane: a membrane (very thin layer) that lets some particles move through it, but prevents others passing through.

plasmolysed: a description of a cell in which the cell membrane has torn away from the cell wall.

turgid: a description of a plant cell that is tight and firm.

turgor pressure: the pressure of the water pushing outwards on a plant cell wall.

water potential gradient: a difference in water potential between two areas.

2 Deduce if there are any anomalous results. If you think there are, draw a ring around them.

3 Draw a line graph of the results, using the axes on Figure 2.2.

TIP

Plot each point as a small, neat cross, ×. Then use a ruler and a sharp pencil to draw straight lines between the points.

Remember to ignore any anomalous results when you draw the lines on your graph.

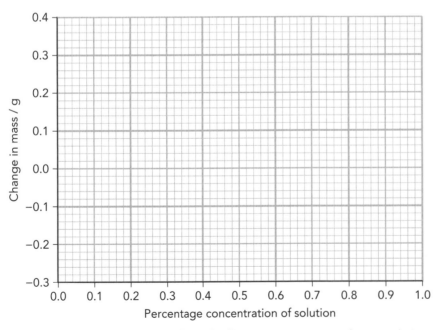

Figure 2.2: Graph showing the effect of different concentrations of sugar solutions.

SELF ASSESSMENT

How confident do you feel about drawing a graph? Give yourself a mark for each item in the checklist. Award yourself:

2 marks   if you did it well

1 mark   if you made a good attempt at it and partly succeeded

0 marks   if you did not try to do it, or did not succeed.

Checklist	Marks awarded
I used a sharp pencil for drawing each cross.	
Each cross is small and neat, and in exactly the right place.	
I used a sharp pencil and ruler to draw the lines.	
Each line goes from exactly the centre of one cross, to exactly the centre of the next cross.	
I ignored any anomalous results when drawing the lines.	
Total (out of 10):	

Practice

4   a   Use your knowledge of osmosis to explain the results of this experiment.
Use ideas about water potential in your answer.

....

....

....

....

....

....

....

b Use the appropriate biological terms to describe each of these.
Choose from:

water potential   flaccid   plasmolysed   osmosis

turgid   turgor pressure

You will not have to use all these terms.

- The condition of the cells in piece A after soaking: ....

- The condition of the cells in piece F after soaking: ....

- What the cell contents are exerting on the cell walls in tissue A

   after soaking: ....

- How the cells in piece F appear under a microscope

   after soaking: ....

5 Suggest how the learner could change his method to get more accurate results.

....

....

....

Challenge

6 The learner's teacher suggested that it would be better if he calculated the percentage change in mass of each piece of potato, rather than just the change in mass. Do you agree? Explain your answer.

....

....

....

....

7 Suggest how the learner could use his results to estimate the concentration of the solution inside the cells in the potato.

....

....

....

....

> Active transport

Exercise 2.3

KEY WORDS

active transport: the movement of molecules or ions through a cell membrane from a region of lower concentration to a region of higher concentration (i.e. against a concentration gradient) using energy from respiration.

Focus

1   Draw lines to match each term with its description.

Term	Description
diffusion	movement of particles through a cell membrane, against a concentration gradient
concentration gradient	a difference in concentration between two places
osmosis	the diffusion of water through a partially permeable membrane
active transport	the net movement of particles down a concentration gradient

Practice

Table 2.3 shows the concentrations of three different ions inside the cells in a plant root and in the water in the soil.

Ion	Concentration in plant root cells/µmol per dm³	Concentration in soil water/µmol per dm³
A	0.5	0.5
B	1.0	0.4
C	0.6	0.8

Table 2.3

2 **a** Identify which ion has the same concentration in the root hair as in the soil water.

....

b Which process is most likely to explain how this ion moves between the root hair and soil water? Circle your answer.

active transport   **diffusion**   **osmosis**

3 Identify which ion has been moved *into* the root hair by active transport. Explain your answer.

....

....

Challenge

4 Suggest and explain *two* advantages to a plant of using active transport to obtain minerals from soil rather than diffusion alone.

i ....

....

ii ....

....

5 If the soil in which the plant is growing is flooded with water, the roots can no longer get enough oxygen.

Suggest how this would affect the concentrations of ions A, B and C in the root cells. Explain each of your suggestions.

....

....

....

....

....

....

....

....

› Chapter 3
Biological molecules
› Carbohydrates, fats and proteins

Exercise 3.1

IN THIS EXERCISE YOU WILL:

- recall which elements make up biological molecules
- compare the numbers and types of elements in biological molecules
- consider the numbers of elements in large, complex molecules.

Focus

1 Glucose has the formula $C_6H_{12}O_6$.

    a How many different elements are in one glucose molecule?

    ....

    b How many of each element are in one glucose molecule?

    ....

2 There are 20 different amino acids.

    One of them, called serine, has the formula $C_3H_7NO_3$.

    a How many different elements are in one serine molecule?

    ....

    b How many of each element are in one serine molecule?

    ....

3 A molecule of glycerol contains carbon and two other elements.
Name these *two* other elements.

    .... and ....

TIP

Remember that the small, subscript number in a formula goes with the element just before that number.

KEY WORDS

amino acids: substances with molecules containing carbon, hydrogen, oxygen and nitrogen; there are 20 different amino acids found in organisms.

antibodies: proteins secreted by white blood cells, which bind to pathogens and help to destroy them.

Benedict's solution: a blue liquid that turns orange-red when heated with reducing sugar.

biuret reagent: a blue solution that turns purple when mixed with amino acids or proteins.

carbohydrates: substances that include sugars, starch and cellulose; they contain carbon, hydrogen and oxygen.

Practice

4   Which two types of molecule contain the same three elements?

Choose *two* from this list:

carbohydrates   water   fats   proteins   amino acids

.... and ....

5   The formula of glucose is given in Question 1.

The formula of another sugar, called ribose, is $C_5H_{10}O_5$.

a   List the differences in the numbers of each element in a molecule of glucose and a molecule of ribose.

....

....

....

b   Another sugar, called glycerone, has the formula $C_3H_8O_3$.

All three sugars, glucose, ribose and glycerone, contain the same elements.

Describe *one* other similarity between the formulas of each of these sugars.

....

....

6   All proteins are made from amino acids that contain the elements carbon, hydrogen, oxygen and nitrogen. Some amino acids contain another element. Name this other element.

....

Challenge

7   Starch is made from many glucose molecules attached together. One particular molecule of starch was found to contain 1800 glucose molecules attached to each other.

Use the formula of glucose in question **1** to calculate the number of carbon atoms in this molecule of starch. Show your working.

....

Exercise 3.2

IN THIS EXERCISE YOU WILL:

- recall which smaller molecules make up larger biological molecules
- think about how larger molecules are made
- consider the numbers of elements in large, complex molecules.

KEY WORDS

reducing sugars: sugars such as glucose, which turn Benedict's solution orange-red when heated together.

starch: a carbohydrate that is used as an energy store in plant cells.

sugars: carbohydrates that have relatively small molecules; they are soluble in water and they taste sweet.

Focus

1   For each of these molecules, name *one* larger biological molecule that can be made from it.

    a   glycerol

    ....

    b   amino acid

    ....

    c   glucose

    ....

    d   fatty acid

    ....

Practice

2   Amino acids are joined together inside cells to make proteins. The amino acids are joined in a chain, end-to-end, with no branches in the chain. The first three amino acids in a protein chain are represented in Figure 3.1.

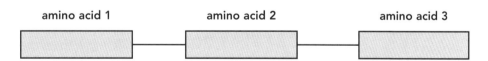

amino acid 1   amino acid 2   amino acid 3

Figure 3.1: The first three amino acids in a protein chain.

The lines between each amino acid represent chemical bonds.

How many of these chemical bonds need to be made in a protein chain containing 120 amino acids?

....

3   When one molecule of a fat is made, three fatty acids are joined to one glycerol molecule. One chemical bond is needed to join each fatty acid to the glycerol.

When each of these chemical bonds is formed, one molecule of water is released.

How many molecules of water will be released when one molecule of this fat is made?

....

Challenge

4   Figure 3.2 shows a type of molecule that is used to make larger biological molecules.

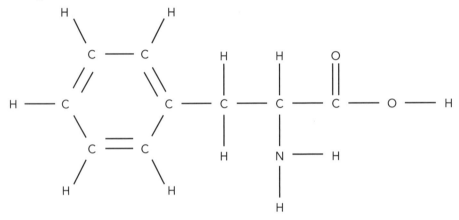

Figure 3.2: Displayed formula of phenylalanine.

Use your understanding of the elements in biological molecules to name this type of molecule.

....

5   Human cells use all 20 amino acids in proteins. However, we only need to take in nine of them in our diet. We do not need to eat foods that contain the other 11 amino acids.

What does this suggest about how we get the other 11 amino acids?

....

....

....

....

Exercise 3.3

IN THIS EXERCISE YOU WILL:

- draw and complete a results chart

- check that you remember information about carbohydrates

- check that you remember how to test for proteins

- recall information about the functions of different parts of cells

- research a protein of your choice

- plan an experiment to test a hypothesis.

Focus

A learner carried out tests on two foods. This is what she wrote in her notebook.

Starch test – food A went brown, food B went black

Benedict's solution – food A went orange-red, food B went blue

1 Draw a results table in the space below and complete it to show the learner's results and conclusions. Think carefully about the best way of showing what she did, what she was testing for, what results she obtained and what these results mean.

> **TIP**
>
> Remember to state the actual colours that the student saw. Do not just write 'no change'. A good phrase to use is 'The solution changed colour from _____ to _____'.

SELF ASSESSMENT

How confident do you feel about drawing and completing a results table? Give yourself a mark for each of the points in the checklist. Award yourself:

2 marks if you did it well

1 mark   if you made a good attempt at it and partly succeeded

0 marks if you did not try to do it, or did not succeed.

Checklist	Marks awarded
I used a ruler and sharp pencil to construct the table.	
I had a row (or column) headed 'Food'.	
I had a row (or column) headed 'Starch test' or 'Iodine test'.	
I had a row (or column) headed 'Reducing sugar test' or 'Benedict's test'.	
I included the starting colour, and the colour it changed to, for each test.	
I included a conclusion for each test, showing whether the starch or reducing sugar was present in the food.	
Total (out of 12):	

2   Complete Table 3.1 about carbohydrates.

Example of carbohydrate	Function in organisms
glucose	
	the form in which plants store energy
cellulose	
glycogen	

Table 3.1

Practice

3 Describe how you would carry out the biuret test, to find out if a substance contains protein.

....

....

....

....

4 **a** Name the part of a cell where proteins are synthesised (made).

....

    b Name the smaller molecules from which proteins are synthesised.

....

    c Explain why the sequence in which these smaller molecules are linked together is important.

....

....

....

5 There are thousands of different proteins in an organism. Choose *one* protein, and use the internet to find out about the function it has.

You could choose a protein from this list, or a different one if you prefer.

antibodies   haemoglobin   insulin

....

....

....

....

....

....

Challenge

6 The biuret test is used to test foods for proteins. The intensity of the colour obtained depends on the concentration of protein in the sample being tested.

Plan an investigation to test this hypothesis:

Milk from cows contains a higher concentration of protein than milk from goats.

Include information about:
- the variables you will change, standardise and measure
- the apparatus and procedure you will use
- predictions of the results you will obtain, if the hypothesis is correct
- an outline results table that you could use.

....

....

....

....

....

....

....

....

....

....

....

....

....

....

....

....

....

....

....

....

> Chapter 4
Enzymes
> Biological catalysts

Exercise 4.1

IN THIS EXERCISE YOU WILL:

- describe what enzymes are
- recall the role of enzymes in organisms
- practise using the correct words to describe how enzymes work.

Focus

1   Use words from this list to complete the sentences in parts **a–e** of this question.
You can use each word once, more than once or not at all.

> **carbohydrate**   **fats and oil**   **water**   **protein**   **fatty acid**
>
> **catalyst**   **speed up**   **slow down**   **get used up**
>
> **stay the same**   **metabolic**   **chemical**   **cells**

a   Enzymes are made from _____ .

b   An enzyme is called a biological _____ .

c   Enzymes are used in all _____ reactions.

d   Enzymes _____ the rate of these reactions.

e   During a reaction involving an enzyme, the enzyme does not _____ .

2   Figure 4.1 shows an enzyme and a molecule of its substrate.
This enzyme is able to split the substrate molecule into two product molecules.

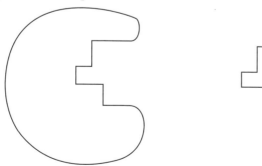

Figure 4.1: An enzyme and a molecule of its substrate.

KEY WORDS

active site: the part of an enzyme molecule to which the substrate temporarily binds.

complementary: with a perfect mirror-image shape.

enzyme–substrate complex: the short-lived structure formed as the substrate binds temporarily to the active site of an enzyme.

enzymes: proteins that are involved in all metabolic reactions, where they function as biological catalysts.

product: the new substance formed by a chemical reaction.

specificity: (of enzymes) only able to act on a particular (specific) substrate.

substrate: the substance that an enzyme acts upon.

On Figure 4.1 label these parts:

- the enzyme
- the active site of the enzyme
- the substrate.

Practice

3   In the space below, draw a diagram of the molecules that will be present after the enzyme in Figure 4.1 has changed the substrate into products.

Challenge

4   Use Figure 4.1 to explain why enzymes are specific to a particular substrate.

....

....

....

....

〉 Factors that affect enzymes

Exercise 4.2

KEY WORDS

optimum: best; for example, the optimum temperature of an enzyme is the temperature at which its activity is greatest.

range: the lowest to the highest value.

Focus

1 Write a multiple-choice question for each of the following sets of answers. Write the correct answer to your question (A, B, C or D) on a separate piece of paper.

a ....

....

....

   A amylase   **B** catalase   **C** lipase   **D** protease

b ....

....

....

   A denatured   **B** killed   **C** slowed down   **D** speeded up

c ....

....

....

   A active   **B** catalyst   **C** chemical   **D** metabolic

2 Write *two* more multiple-choice questions about enzymes. For each question, give four answers to choose from – A, B, C or D. Write the correct answers to your questions on a separate piece of paper.

a ....

....

....

....

....

....

b ....

....

....

....

....

....

PEER ASSESSMENT

Exchange your questions with a partner.

Can you answer their questions correctly? Did they word their questions clearly?

Can they answer your questions correctly? Did you word your questions clearly, so that your partner understood and could choose the correct answer?

Practice

A student carried out an experiment to investigate the effect of temperature on the enzyme lipase. Lipase digests fats to fatty acids and glycerol. Fatty acids have a low pH.

The student made a solution of lipase and added equal volumes of it to five test-tubes. The student treated the tubes as shown in Figure 4.2.

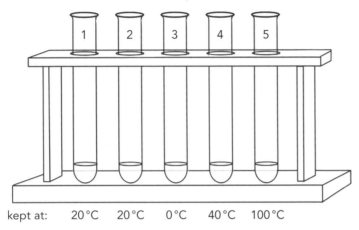

kept at: 20 °C   20 °C   0 °C   40 °C   100 °C

Figure 4.2: Solutions of lipase in test-tubes kept at different temperatures.

The student:

*   kept all five tubes at these temperatures for five minutes
*   used a pH meter to measure the pH of the liquid in each tube
*   added equal volumes of milk (which contains fat) to tubes 2, 3, 4 and 5
*   measured the pH of the contents of each tube, every two minutes.

    The results are shown in Table 4.1.

Tube	1	2	3	4	5
Temp / °C	20				
Milk added?		yes			
pH at:					
0 mins	7.0	7.0	7.0	7.0	7.0
2 mins	7.0	6.8	7.0	6.7	7.0
4 mins	7.0	6.7	7.0	6.5	7.0
6 mins	7.0	6.6	7.0	6.3	7.0
8 mins	7.0	6.6	6.9	6.2	7.0
10 mins	7.0	6.5	6.9	6.2	7.0

Table 4.1

3   What is the substrate of the enzyme lipase?

....

4   What are the products when lipase acts on its substrate?

....

5   Explain why the pH becomes lower when lipase acts on its substrate.

....

....

6   Complete Table 4.1 by filling in all of the blank boxes.

7   Explain why the pH did not change in tube 1.

....

8   a   Explain why the pH did not change in tube 5.

....

    b   Explain what has happened to the enzyme in tube 5 and how this affects the
        result seen in this tube.

....

....

....

....

9   Explain why the results for tubes 2 and 3 differed from each other.

....

....

....

....

....

> **TIP**
>
> The information to help you to do this is in the descriptions near the start of the question.

10 The student concluded that the optimum temperature for lipase is 40 °C.
Evaluate the evidence for this conclusion. Explain your answer.

....

....

....

....

....

11 Suggest some changes that could be made to this experiment to obtain a more
accurate value for the optimum temperature of lipase.

....

....

....

....

Challenge

12 The pH of a liquid can be kept constant by adding a buffer solution to it. You can
obtain buffer solutions for any pH value you require. You can use a pH meter to
measure the pH.

   a Explain, in terms of enzyme structure and function, why a constant pH is
useful for an enzyme investigation.

....

....

....

....

b Plan an investigation to test this hypothesis:

The optimum pH for amylase is 7.5.

Figure 4.3 shows some of the apparatus you might like to include.

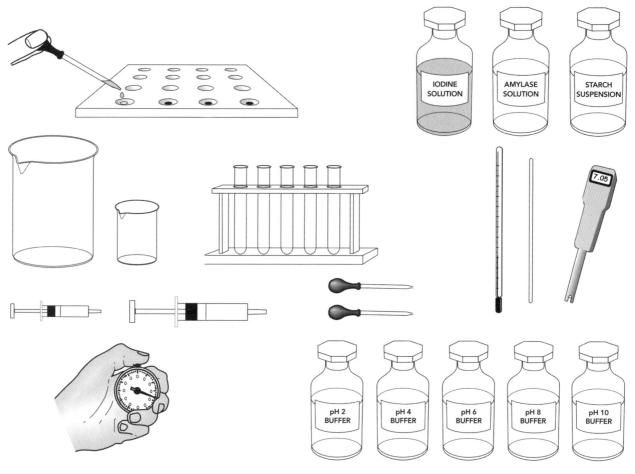

Figure 4.3: A selection of apparatus.

i What will you vary in your experiment?

....

ii Over what range will you vary it?

....

iii How will you vary it?

....

....

iv   What variables will you keep constant in your experiment? How will you do this?

....

....

....

v   What results will you measure in your experiment? How will you measure them and when?

....

....

....

....

vi   Briefly outline the steps you will follow in your investigation.

....

....

....

....

....

....

....

....

....

....

c   In the space below, draw a results table in which you could record
    your results.

d   On the grid below, sketch a graph to show the results you would expect if the
    hypothesis is correct. Remember to label the axes.

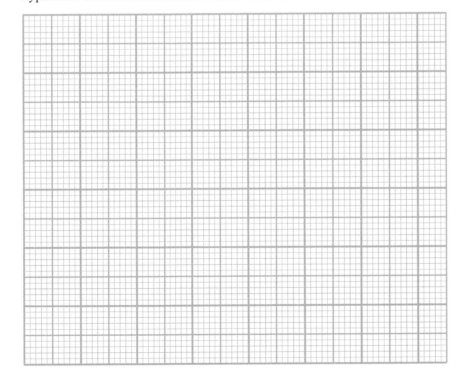

> **TIP**
>
> When you are asked
> to sketch a graph,
> draw two axes and
> label them. You do
> not need to add a
> scale to either axis.
> Then draw a line
> that is the shape you
> would expect
> to obtain.

SELF ASSESSMENT

How confident do you feel about planning an experiment? Give yourself a mark for each of the points in the checklist. Award yourself:

2 marks if you did it well

1 mark if you made a good attempt at it and partly succeeded

0 marks if you did not try to do it, or did not succeed.

Now ask your teacher to mark you.

Checklist	Marks awarded	
	You	Teacher
I can state the variable to be changed (independent variable), the range of this variable and how I will vary it.		
I can state at least three important variables to be kept constant (and not include ones that are not important).		
I can state the variable to be measured (dependent variable), how I will measure it and when I will measure it.		
I can draw a clear results table into which I can write my results.		
I can predict what the results will be if the hypothesis is correct.		
Total (out of 10):		

If you (or your teacher) awarded fewer than 10 marks, what could you do better if you did a similar task in future?

....

....

....

> Chapter 5

Plant nutrition

> ## Photosynthesis

Exercise 5.1

IN THIS EXERCISE YOU WILL:

- describe the process of photosynthesis
- summarise the sources of the raw materials of photosynthesis, as well as its products
- describe the role of chlorophyll in photosynthesis
- list some uses for glucose and other substances within a plant.

KEY WORDS

chlorophyll: a green pigment (coloured substance) that absorbs energy from light; the energy is used to combine carbon dioxide with water to make glucose.

nectar: a sweet liquid secreted by many insect-pollinated flowers, to attract their pollinators.

photosynthesis: the process by which plants synthesise carbohydrates from raw materials using energy from light.

sucrose: a sugar whose molecules are made of glucose and another similar molecule (fructose) linked together.

Focus

1   Write the word equation for photosynthesis.

   ....

2   Describe how a leaf obtains the two substances on the left-hand side of your equation.

   ....

   ....

3   Describe what happens to the two substances on the right-hand side of your equation.

   ....

   ....

Practice

4   Explain the difference between each of these pairs of terms.

   a   Chloroplast and chlorophyll

   ....

   ....

TIP

If you are asked to write a word equation, do *not* use formulae or write a balanced equation.

b   Organic substances and inorganic substances

....

....

5   Describe the role of chlorophyll in photosynthesis.

....

....

6   Glucose that is made in photosynthesis can be stored as starch or changed to another sugar for transport in phloem.

Give *three* other uses for glucose in plants.

i   ....

ii   ....

iii ....

7   Complete Table 5.1 to show how, and for what purpose, plants obtain these substances.

	Obtained from	Used for
Nitrate ions		
Water		
Magnesium ions		
Carbon dioxide		

Table 5.1

Challenge

8   **a**   Write the balanced symbol equation for photosynthesis.

....

b   Name the carbohydrate that is transported in the phloem of plants.

....

9   Figure 5.1 shows a palisade cell. (It is a little unusual, as it has a strand of cytoplasm across the middle of the cell.)

Write short descriptions in each box, to explain how a palisade cell in a leaf gets what it needs for photosynthesis, and what happens to the products.

Use each of these words at least once.

air spaces   diffusion   epidermis   osmosis   phloem

xylem   root hair   starch   stomata   sucrose   transparent

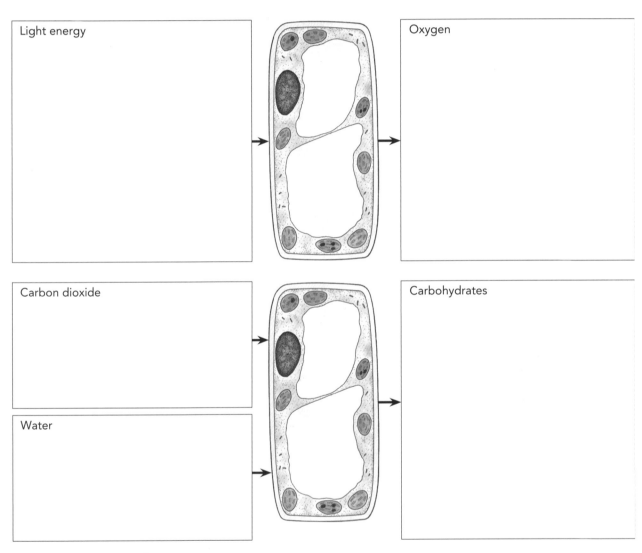

Light energy

Oxygen

Carbon dioxide

Carbohydrates

Water

Figure 5.1: A palisade cell.

〉 Leaves

Exercise 5.2

IN THIS EXERCISE YOU WILL:

- describe the structure of a leaf

- identify the positions of tissues in a leaf and describe their functions

- look carefully at unfamiliar diagrams, make comparisons, and use what you can see to suggest answers to questions

- explain how leaves are adapted for photosynthesis.

KEY WORDS

cuticle: a thin layer of wax that covers the upper surface of a leaf.

palisade mesophyll: the layer of cells immediately beneath the upper epidermis, where most photosynthesis happens.

spongy mesophyll: the layer of cells immediately beneath the palisade mesophyll, where some photosynthesis happens; this tissue contains a lot of air spaces between the cells.

Focus

1   Explain the difference between each of these pairs of terms.

   a   Palisade mesophyll and spongy mesophyll

      ....

      ....

   b   Guard cell and stoma

      ....

      ....

Practice

Some of the leaves on a tree spend most of the day in bright sunlight, while others are in the shade. The diagrams in Figure 5.2 show sections through a leaf growing in the sunlight and a leaf growing in the shade.

a

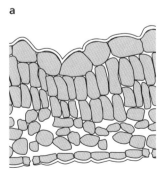

sun leaf

b

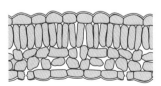

shade leaf

Figure 5.2 a: Section of a leaf growing in the sunlight. **b:** Section of a leaf growing in the shade.

2   On the *shade leaf* diagram (Figure 5.2b), label these tissues:

lower epidermis   palisade mesophyll

spongy mesophyll   upper epidermis

3   On the *shade leaf* diagram (Figure 5.2b), draw a few spots in each cell that you would expect to contain chloroplasts.

4   Use the diagram of the *sun leaf* (Figure 5.2a) to explain *three* ways in which this leaf is adapted for photosynthesis.

i   ....

....

....

ii   ....

....

....

iii   ....

....

....

> **KEY WORD**
>
> **stomata (singular: stoma):** openings in the surface of a leaf, most commonly in the lower surface; they are surrounded by pairs of guard cells, which control whether the stomata are open or closed.

Challenge

5   Complete Table 5.2 to compare the structures of each of these parts of the leaves shown in Figure 5.2.

Part of leaf	Sun leaf	Shade leaf
Cuticle		
Palisade mesophyll		
Spongy mesophyll		

Table 5.2

> **TIP**
>
> When you make comparisons, include comparative words such as 'thicker'.

6   Suggest an explanation for the difference in the cuticle that you have described in Table 5.2.

....

....

7   Suggest an explanation for the difference in the palisade layer that you have described in Table 5.2.

....

....

....

....

TIP

Do not panic when you see the command word 'suggest'. Think about what you know, then try to apply that to the situation you are being asked about.

> Factors affecting photosynthesis
Exercise 5.3

IN THIS EXERCISE YOU WILL:

- practise drawing a line graph
- use lines on a graph to interpret the factors affecting the rate of photosynthesis
- use your understanding of limiting factors to make a recommendation.

KEY WORDS

arbitrary units: sometimes used on a graph scale to represent quantitative differences between values, instead of 'real' units such as seconds or centimetres; this is usually because the real units would be very complicated to use.

Focus

An experiment was performed to find out how fast a plant photosynthesised as the concentration of carbon dioxide in the air around it was varied. The results are shown in Table 5.3.

Percentage concentration of carbon dioxide	Rate of photosynthesis / arbitrary units
0.00	0
0.02	33
0.04	53
0.06	68
0.08	79
0.10	86

(continued)

Percentage concentration of carbon dioxide	Rate of photosynthesis / arbitrary units
0.12	89
0.14	90
0.16	90
0.18	90
0.20	90

Table 5.3

1   Plot these results on the grid below and draw a line.

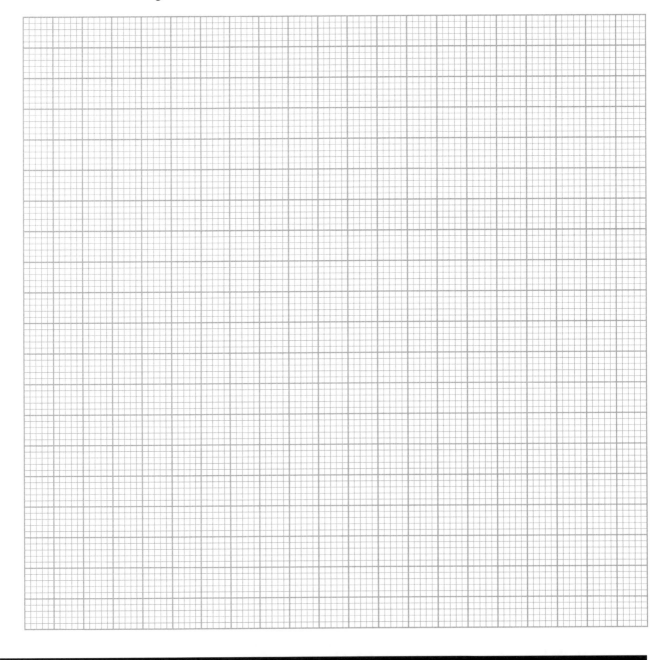

PEER ASSESSMENT

Exchange your graph with a partner. Give them a mark for each of the points in the checklist. When you swap back, write the marks you would give yourself in the last column. Are there any differences between the two marks? If so, why are the marks different?

For each point, award:

2 marks   if it was done really well

1 mark   if a good attempt was made

0 marks   if it was not attempted.

Checklist	Marks awarded	
	Your partner	You
You have drawn the axes with a ruler, and used most of the width and height of the graph paper for the axis labels.		
You have used a good scale for the x-axis and the y-axis, going up in intervals of 10 on the y-axis, and 0.02 on the x-axis.		
You have included the correct unit with the scale that requires one.		
You have plotted each point precisely and correctly.		
You have used a small, neat cross for each point.		
You have drawn a single, clear line – either by ruling a line between each pair of points, or drawing a well-positioned best-fit line.		
Total (out of 12):		

2   Explain why the rate of photosynthesis increases as carbon dioxide concentration increases.

   ....

   ....

Practice

3 The experiment was repeated at a lower light intensity. The results are shown in Table 5.4.

Plot these values on your graph in question **1** and draw a line. Label the two lines.

Percentage concentration of carbon dioxide	Rate of photosynthesis / arbitrary units
0.00	0
0.02	20
0.04	29
0.06	35
0.08	39
0.10	42
0.12	45
0.14	46
0.16	46
0.18	46
0.20	46

Table 5.4

4 State the carbon dioxide concentration of normal air.

....

5 Use your graph from question **1** to determine the rate of photosynthesis in normal air in higher light intensity.

....

Challenge

6   Farmers and market gardeners often add carbon dioxide to the air in glasshouses where crops are growing. Use your graph from question **1** to explain the advantage of doing this.

....

....

....

....

7   It is expensive to add carbon dioxide to glasshouses. Suggest a suitable concentration of carbon dioxide to add to a glasshouse in high light intensity, to obtain a good financial return from the sale of the crop. Explain your answer.

....

....

....

....

> Chapter 6
Human nutrition

> Diet

Exercise 6.1

IN THIS EXERCISE YOU WILL:

- practise finding and using relevant data in a table.

Table 6.1 shows the energy and nutrients contained in 100 g of five foods.

Food	Energy/kJ	Protein/g	Fat/g	Carbohydrate/g	Calcium/mg	Iron/mg	Vitamin C/mg	Vitamin D/mg
apple	150	0.2	0.0	9.0	0	0.2	2	0.0
chicken, roast	630	25.0	5.0	0.0	0	0.8	0	0.0
egg, scrambled	1050	10.0	23.0	0.0	60	2.0	0	1.8
rice, boiled	500	2.0	0.3	30.0	0	0.0	0	0.0
spinach, boiled	130	5.0	0.5	1.5	600	4.0	25	0.0

Table 6.1

Focus

1   Which food contains the most energy per 100 g?

   ....

2   Which nutrients in the table provide energy?

   ....

3   Which nutrients in the table are mineral ions?

   ....

KEY WORDS

balanced diet: a diet that contains all of the required nutrients, in suitable proportions, and the right amount of energy.

diet: the food eaten in one day.

4   How many times more protein does roast chicken contain, than boiled rice?
    Show your working.

    ....

Practice

5   What pattern can you see in the foods in Table 6.1 that contain carbohydrate?

    ....

    ....

6   Scrambled egg has the highest energy content per gram of all of the foods in the
    table. What data in Table 6.1 could explain why the energy content of scrambled
    egg is so high?

    ....

    ....

7   A girl has anaemia. Which foods from the table would be most helpful for her to
    include in her diet? Explain your answer.

    ....

    ....

Challenge

8   Use the data in Table 6.1 to determine which of the five foods contains the greatest
    mass of water per 100 g. Show your working.

    ....

> The digestive system
Exercise 6.2

IN THIS EXERCISE YOU WILL:

- check that you understand the meanings of some terms relating to digestion and absorption
- add annotations to the correct part of a diagram of the digestive system
- describe the role of bile in digestion.

Focus

1 Draw lines to match each term with its description.

Term	Description
pancreas	the breakdown of food into small molecules so that they can move from the intestine into the blood
absorption	an organ that secretes a juice containing hydrochloric acid
duodenum	the movement of nutrient molecules and ions through the wall of the intestine into the blood
stomach	the part of the alimentary canal into which bile and pancreatic juice flow
digestion	an organ that produces enzymes that digest starch, protein and fat

Practice

2 With the aid of examples wherever possible, explain the differences between each of the following pairs of terms.

a Digestion and absorption ....

....

b Small intestine and large intestine ....

....

KEY WORDS

absorption: the movement of nutrients from the alimentary canal into the blood.

digestion: the breakdown of food.

duodenum: the first part of the small intestine, into which the pancreatic duct and bile duct empty fluids.

gall bladder: a small organ that stores bile, before the bile is released into the duodenum.

pancreas: a creamy-white organ lying close to the stomach, which secretes pancreatic juice; it also secretes the hormones insulin and glucagon, which are involved in the control of blood glucose concentration.

salivary glands: groups of cells close to the mouth, which secrete saliva into the salivary ducts.

small intestine: a long, narrow part of the alimentary canal, consisting of the duodenum and ileum.

c   Duodenum and ileum ....

....

d   Salivary gland and pancreas ....

....

Challenge

3   Figure 6.1 shows the human digestive system.

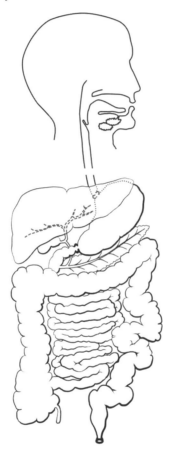

Figure 6.1: The human digestive system.

Add each label to the appropriate part of the diagram. One of the labels should be written in *two* places.

Labels to add:

- physical digestion increases the surface area of food (*two* places)
- acid is neutralised here
- the gall bladder
- secretes a liquid with a low pH, which kills bacteria
- bile is made.

SELF ASSESSMENT

How confident do you feel about labelling a diagram of the digestive system? Give yourself a rating for each of the points in the checklist, using:

☺ if you did it really well

😐 if you made a good attempt at it and partly succeeded

☹ if you did not try to do it, or did not succeed.

Checklist	Rating
I drew the label lines with a ruler.	
Each label line touched the structure I meant to label.	
The label lines did not cross.	
The labels were written alongside the diagram, not on top of it.	
I got all six of the labels correct.	

4   Describe the *two* roles of bile in the digestive system.

i   ....

   ....

ii   ....

   ....

Exercise 6.3

IN THIS EXERCISE YOU WILL:

- explain why enzymes are needed in digestion
- describe the actions of the digestive enzymes
- describe where each digestive enzyme acts.

Focus

1 Explain why enzymes are needed in digestion.

....

....

....

....

....

Practice

2 Complete Table 6.2 to show the names and functions of the digestive enzymes.

Name of enzyme	Acts on	Produces
	starch	
protease		
	fats and oils	

Table 6.2

Challenge

3 For each of the enzymes in question **2**, state where it is produced and where it acts in the digestive system. Remember that some enzymes are produced and act in more than one place.

The enzyme _____ is produced in _____ and acts in _____

The enzyme _____ is produced in _____ and acts in _____

The enzyme _____ is produced in _____ and acts in _____

〉 Digestion

Exercise 6.4

IN THIS EXERCISE YOU WILL:

- explain the importance of digestion
- practise describing what is shown in a graph
- apply your understanding of diet, digestion and absorption to a new context.

KEY WORDS

bile: an alkaline fluid produced by the liver, which helps with fat digestion.

bile duct: the tube that carries bile from the gall bladder to the duodenum.

Focus

1 Explain why starch is digested by the body.

....

....

....

Practice

2 In an experiment, a starch-digesting enzyme was added to a starch suspension in a test-tube at 35 °C.

The graph in Figure 6.2 shows how the amount of starch remaining in the test-tube changed over the next eight minutes.

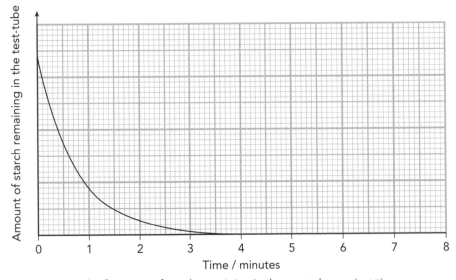

Figure 6.2: Graph of amount of starch remaining in the test-tube against time.

a State the time at which the rate of digestion of starch was fastest.

....

b Name the product of the digestion of starch in this test-tube.

....

c On Figure 6.2 sketch a line to show the result that would be expected if the experiment was repeated at 25 °C.

Challenge

In an investigation into the absorption of vitamin D from the alimentary canal, a volunteer ate a measured quantity of vitamin D on a piece of toast. Blood samples were then taken from him at intervals over a period of 72 hours, and the concentration of vitamin D in each blood sample was measured.

The results are shown in the graph in Figure 6.3.

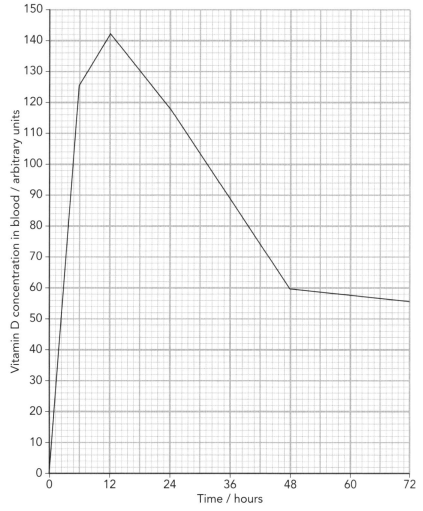

Figure 6.3: Graph of vitamin D concentration in blood, over 72 hours.

3 Describe the changes in the concentration of vitamin D in the blood over the 72-hour period (using the Tip box to help you).

....

....

....

....

....

TIP

When you describe a line graph, try to include:

- what happens to the value on the *y*-axis, when the *x*-axis value increases (that is, state a general trend)

- where the maximum or minimum values of the line occur, giving both the *x*-axis and *y*-axis values and their units

- anywhere that the direction or gradient of the line changes, quoting the *x*-axis and *y*-axis values where this happens, including their units

- a calculation – for example, the difference between the concentrations at two points on the graph.

---

4 Calculate the percentage change in vitamin D concentration between 12 hours and 48 hours. Show your working. Give your answer to the nearest whole number.

....

TIP

$$\text{percentage change} = \frac{\text{change in value}}{\text{original value}} \times 100$$

---

5   Name the part of the alimentary canal in which vitamin D is absorbed into the blood.

....

6   Explain how this part of the alimentary canal is adapted to make absorption efficient.

....

....

....

....

....

7   Explain why vitamin D does not need to be digested before it is absorbed.

....

....

8   Vitamin D is soluble in fat, but insoluble in water. It is present in the fat component of foods that we eat. Use this information to suggest how bile helps us to absorb vitamin D from food.

....

....

....

9   The volunteer was asked not to expose his skin to sunlight during the investigation. Suggest why this was done.

....

....

....

Chapter 7

Transport

> Transport in plants

Exercise 7.1

IN THIS EXERCISE YOU WILL:

- check that you know the functions of xylem and phloem
- practise identifying tissues and calculating magnification
- link the structure of xylem to its functions
- make and label biological drawings.

KEY WORDS

phloem: a plant tissue that transports substances made by the plant, such as sucrose and amino acids.

sink: part of a plant to which sucrose or amino acids are being transported, and where they are used or stored.

source: part of a plant that releases sucrose or amino acids, to be transported to other parts.

xylem: a plant tissue that transports water and mineral ions and helps to support the plant.

Focus

1   Complete the sentences, using words from the list.

> **amino acids   fatty acids   leaves   mineral ions**
>
> **organ   roots   sucrose   tissue   water**

Xylem is a _____ that transports _____ and _____ _____ from the _____ of a plant to its _____.

Phloem transports _____ _____ and _____ from the leaves to other parts of the plant.

Practice

2   Figure 7.1 shows part of a buttercup root, seen using the high-power lens of a light microscope.

Use ruled lines to label these tissues:

> **cortex   phloem   xylem**

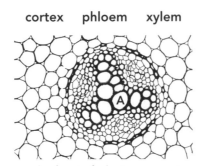

Figure 7.1: Photomicrograph of part of a buttercup root.

3   The magnification of the image in Figure 7.1 is ×200.

Calculate the actual diameter of the cell labelled **A**.

Show your working. Give your answer in millimetres.

....

Challenge

4   Figure 7.2 shows a transverse section of a stem, and a transverse section of a root.

Figure 7.2: A transverse section of a stem, and a transverse section of a root.

a   Explain what is meant by the term *transverse section*.

....

....

b   In the space below, make a copy of Figure 7.2 that shows a transverse section of a stem. Label the xylem tissue.

c In the space below, make a copy of Figure 7.2 that shows a transverse section of a root. Label the xylem tissue.

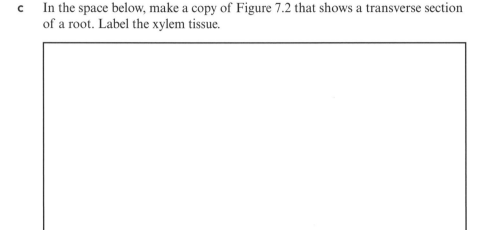

d On your two diagrams, label the position of the phloem tissue.

Exercise 7.2

IN THIS EXERCISE YOU WILL:

- describe the structure of root hair cells

- link the structure of root hair cells to their function

- think about factors that affect the rate of water uptake

- calculate the size of a root hair cell.

Focus

1 Figure 7.3 is a photograph that shows part of a plant root, taken through a light microscope. A root hair cell can be seen in the photograph.

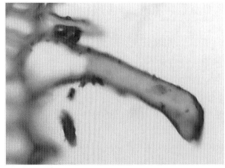

Figure 7.3: Part of a plant root.

a In the space below, make a drawing of the root hair cell. Do not include any other cells.

TIP

When you make a biological drawing, remember to use single, complete lines and do not use any shading.

b On your drawing, label:

- the cell wall

- the cytoplasm.

2 Name *two* things that root hair cells take in from the soil.

i ....

ii ....

Practice

3 Describe *two* differences you would expect between the structure of a root hair cell and a cell in the leaf that is adapted for photosynthesis.

i ....

ii ....

4 One of the functions of plant roots is to take in water. Much of this water is lost through the leaves.

a Name the process by which plants lose water through the leaves.

....

b List the factors that affect the rate of this process.

....

Challenge

5 a Measure the length of the root hair cell in the photograph. Measure along its maximum length. Give your answer in mm.

....

b The magnification of this photograph is ×200. Calculate the actual length of the cell.

Show your working and give your answer in mm.

....

c Convert the actual length of the cell into µm. Show your working.

....

> **TIP**
>
> There are 1000 µm in 1 mm, so to convert from mm to µm simply multiply by 1000. To convert from µm to mm, divide by 1000.

6 A root hair cell has a large surface area. Describe how this adaptation is related to its function.

....

....

....

SELF ASSESSMENT

How confident do you feel about your calculation of the actual length (in micrometres) of the root hair cell in the photograph? Give yourself a rating for each of the points in the checklist, using:

☺ if you did it really well

😐 if you made a good attempt at it and partly succeeded

☹ if you did not try to do it, or did not succeed.

Checklist	Rating
I measured along the maximum length of the root hair cell in the photograph.	
I used the magnification of the photograph to calculate the actual length of the cell.	
I converted the actual length of the cell into micrometres and showed my working.	

Exercise 7.3

IN THIS EXERCISE YOU WILL:

- apply your understanding of sources and sinks to a new situation
- practise describing numerical results in words
- suggest explanations for results.

An experiment was carried out in Switzerland to investigate the movement of carbohydrates from sources to sinks in pine trees, *Pinus cembra*. Switzerland is a mountainous country in Europe.

Pine trees are coniferous trees, which keep their leaves all through the winter.

Focus

1 In which form are carbohydrates transported in phloem? Draw a (circle) around the correct answer.

> **glucose   starch   sucrose**

2 In which form are carbohydrates stored in plant cells? Draw a (circle) around the correct answer.

> **glucose   starch   sucrose**

3 In spring and summer in Switzerland, the leaves of pine trees photosynthesise.

Suggest *two* reasons why pine trees photosynthesise in spring and summer in Switzerland, but not in winter.

i ....

ii ....

Practice

4 Would you expect the leaves to be sources or sinks in spring and summer? Explain your answer.

....

....

....

5 Would you expect the leaves to be sources or sinks in winter? Explain your answer.

....

....

....

Table 7.1 shows the amount of starch, measured as a percentage of the dry mass of the tissues, in the leaves and roots of pine trees at three times of year.

Time of year	Starch in leaves/percentage of dry mass	Starch in roots/percentage of dry mass
spring	15.0	2.6
summer	15.6	3.1
autumn	4.9	4.1

Table 7.1

6 Describe the changes in the amount of starch in the pine tree *leaves* from spring until autumn.

....

....

....

TIP

Remember not to include reasons when you are asked to 'describe'.

7 Describe the changes in the amount of starch in the pine tree *roots* from spring until autumn.

....

....

....

8 Suggest reasons for the changes described in your answers to questions **6** and **7**.

....

....

....

....

....

Challenge

9 In summer, the researchers removed the buds from some pine trees, and the leaves from other pine trees. They left some pine trees untreated, to act as controls.

They measured the amount of starch in the leaves and buds of each group of trees at the end of the summer.

Their results are shown in Table 7.2.

Treatment	Starch in leaves/percentage of dry mass	Starch in buds/percentage of dry mass
control	4.9	7.1
buds removed	4.9	
leaves removed		6.5

Table 7.2

Describe *and* explain the results shown in the table.

....

....

....

....

....

....

....

....

....

....

⟩ Transport in animals

Exercise 7.4

IN THIS EXERCISE YOU WILL:

- check your understanding of the basic structure of the human circulatory system

- interpret information about the heart from a graph

- explain the advantages of a double circulation.

Focus

1 Complete the following sentences about the human circulatory system using the words below. Not all words need to be used.

    arteries   veins   capillaries   pump   valves   blood vessels

The circulatory system is a system of _____

in which blood is transported.

The heart acts as a _____ to move the blood.

There are _____ in the circulatory system, which ensure a

one-way flow of blood.

2 Figure 7.4 shows a simple plan of the human circulatory system.

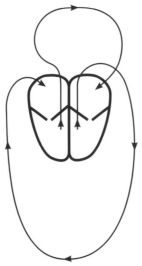

Figure 7.4: A simple plan of the human circulatory system.

KEY WORDS

aorta: the largest artery in the body, which receives oxygenated blood from the left ventricle and delivers it to the body organs.

atria: the thin-walled chambers at the top of the heart, which receive blood.

circulatory system: a system of blood vessels with a pump and valves to ensure one-way flow of blood.

deoxygenated blood: blood containing only a little oxygen.

double circulatory system: a system in which blood passes through the heart twice on one complete circuit of the body.

haemoglobin: a red pigment found in red blood cells, which can combine reversibly with oxygen; it is a protein.

oxygenated blood: blood containing a lot of oxygen.

On Figure 7.4:

- shade in red the parts of the heart that contain oxygenated blood
- shade in blue the parts that contain deoxygenated blood.

Practice

3   Figure 7.5 shows how the volume of the left ventricle changes over a time period of 1.6 seconds.

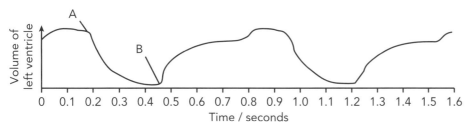

Figure 7.5: How the volume of the left ventricle changes over a time period of 1.6 seconds.

a   How many complete heart beats are shown in Figure 7.5?

....

b   i   Use Figure 7.5 to calculate how long one heart beat takes. Show your working.

....

ii   Use your answer to **b i** to calculate the heart rate in beats per minute. Show your working.

....

c   Describe what is happening between points A and B in Figure 7.5.

....

....

....

KEY WORDS

pathogens: microorganisms that cause disease.

plasma: the liquid part of blood.

platelets: tiny cell fragments present in blood, which help with clotting.

pulmonary artery: the artery that carries deoxygenated blood from the right ventricle to the lungs.

pulmonary veins: the veins that carry oxygenated blood from the lungs to the left atrium of the heart.

red blood cells: biconcave blood cells with no nucleus, which transport oxygen.

single circulatory system: a system in which blood passes through the heart only once on one complete circuit of the body.

valves: structures that allow a liquid to flow in one direction only.

vena cava: the large vein that brings deoxygenated blood to the right atrium.

d Describe how the valves between the atria and ventricles help to ensure a one-way flow of blood through the heart.

....

....

....

e On the graph grid below, make a copy of the graph in Figure 7.5. On your graph, sketch a line to show the volume of the right ventricle during this time period.

KEY WORDS

ventricles: the thick-walled chambers at the base of the heart, which pump out blood.

white blood cells: blood cells with a nucleus, which help to defend against pathogens.

Challenge

4 Many animals with double circulatory systems have higher metabolic rates than those with single circulatory systems. Suggest an explanation for this.

....

....

....

....

....

....

Exercise 7.5

IN THIS EXERCISE YOU WILL:

- practise identifying features of blood vessels

- check that you remember the functions of the different components of blood

- practise naming the parts of the heart and describing their functions

- practise reading new information carefully

- apply your knowledge of the human circulatory system in a new context.

Focus

1   Complete Table 7.3 by placing a tick (✓) or cross (✗) in each space. One row has been done for you.

Feature	Arteries	Veins	Capillaries
contain valves			
wall is one cell thick			
carry blood at high pressure	✓	✗	✗
have a wide lumen			

Table 7.3

2   Draw *one* line from each component (part) of blood to its function.

Component	Function
red blood cells	transport nutrients
plasma	destroy pathogens
white blood cells	clotting
platelets	transport oxygen

Practice

Figure 7.6 shows a section through a human heart.

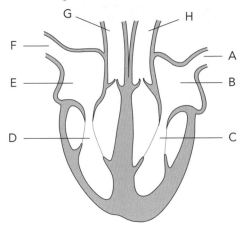

Figure 7.6: A section through a human heart.

3   Write the letter of each structure from Figure 7.6 in Table 7.4. The first one has been done for you. Then complete the table by writing the function of each structure.

Structure	Letter	Function
aorta	H	transports oxygenated blood to body cells
right ventricle		
left atrium		
left ventricle		
right atrium		
pulmonary artery		
pulmonary vein		
vena cava		

Table 7.4

Challenge

Figure 7.7 shows the heart of a fetus (a baby that is still developing in its mother's uterus).

In a fetus, the lungs do not work. The fetus gets its oxygen from the mother, to whom it is connected by the umbilical cord. This cord contains a vein, which carries the oxygenated blood to the fetus's vena cava.

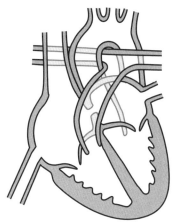

Figure 7.7: The heart of a fetus.

4   On Figure 7.7, write the letter **O** in the chamber of the heart that first receives oxygenated blood in an adult person.

5   On Figure 7.7, write the letters **OF** in the chamber of the heart that first receives oxygenated blood in a fetus.

6   If you look carefully at Figure 7.7, you can see that there is a hole in the septum between the left and right atria. Suggest the function of this hole in the heart of a fetus.

....

....

....

....

7   When the baby is born, it takes its first breath. The hole in the septum of the heart quickly closes.

Explain why this is important.

....

....

....

....

Exercise 7.6

IN THIS EXERCISE YOU WILL:

- recall ways of monitoring heart rate
- think about what happens to heart rate during exercise
- interpret information about heart rate from graphs
- explain and compare different people's heart rates during exercise.

Focus

1   Our heart rate is not constant. It varies during the day according to a number of different factors.

Write down *two* ways in which our heart rate can be monitored.

i   ....

ii ....

2   Two people, A and B, had their heart rates monitored before, during and after exercise (recovery). The results are shown in Figure 7.8.

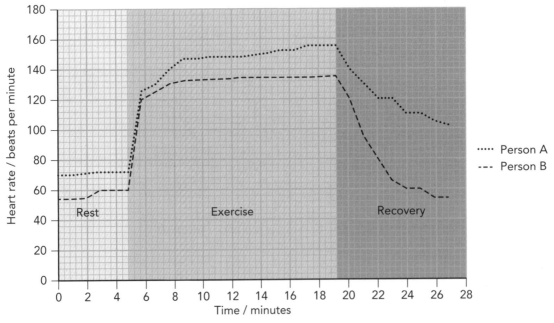

Figure 7.8: Monitoring heart rate.

a Describe the general trend in the heart rates of both people as shown in Figure 7.8. You do *not* need to compare the two people.

....

....

....

....

TIP

When describing patterns in graphs, you should include values from the graph. To do this, read values off both axes to improve your answer.

Practice

b One of the people, A or B, had done training for several weeks before this exercise. State which person had done this training and explain your answer.

Person: ....

Reason: ....

....

....

Challenge

c During the exercise, the muscles of person A and person B both require the same volume of blood every minute. What does this suggest about the structures of the hearts of person A and person B?

....

....

....

Exercise 7.7

IN THIS EXERCISE YOU WILL:

- consider the factors that increase the risk of coronary heart disease
- think of how to reduce the risk of coronary heart disease
- interpret information about heart disease from a table.

Focus

1 There are several risk factors for coronary heart disease (CHD).

  a Describe what is meant by a risk factor.

  ....

  ....

  b One of the risk factors for CHD is lack of exercise. List *three* other risk factors for CHD.

  i ....

  ii ....

  iii ....

Practice

2 Imagine you are a doctor.

  A person comes to see you. They are overweight, partly because they have difficulty exercising because of mobility issues. They are also a smoker. They are male and 47 years old.

  Plan what advice you would give this person to reduce their risk of CHD.

  Remember to keep the advice as simple as possible.

  ....

  ....

  ....

  ....

  ....

  ....

Challenge

3 Deaths from CHD vary around the world.

Table 7.5 shows the number of deaths from CHD per 100 000 people in some countries in 2020.

Country	Number of deaths per 100 000 population
Tajikistan	389.75
Morocco	242.07
Hungary	155.07
Cambodia	109.52
Mexico	92.41
Kenya	72.70
South Korea	27.78

Table 7.5 *Source:* Data taken from WHO 2020 facts summarised at
https://www.worldlifeexpectancy.com/cause-of-death/coronary-heart-disease/by-country/

a Explain why the numbers in Table 7.5 for each country are given as deaths per 100 000 population and not total number of deaths.

....

....

....

b A student looks at Table 7.5 and says: "More people in Hungary die from CHD than in Mexico." Discuss whether this statement is true.

....

....

....

....

c Suggest some other information that could be included with these numbers in order to allow a more valid comparison to be made between these countries with regard to CHD.

....

....

....

....

d People in different countries have different risk factors for CHD. Suggest one other factor that could cause varying numbers of deaths per 100 000 people in different countries.

....

....

Exercise 7.8

IN THIS EXERCISE YOU WILL:

- list the components of blood
- describe the functions of the components of blood
- practise recognising different types of blood cell
- practise recognising different types of white blood cell
- describe the functions of different types of white blood cell.

Focus

1 One of the components of blood is red blood cells. List *three* other components of blood.

i ....

ii ....

iii ....

Practice

2 Describe the functions of the following:

a Red blood cells – give *one* function

....

....

b Plasma – give *three* functions.

i ....

ii ....

iii ....

3   The figures in Table 7.6 show two types of blood cell, **a** and **b**, found in blood.
    Name each of these cells.

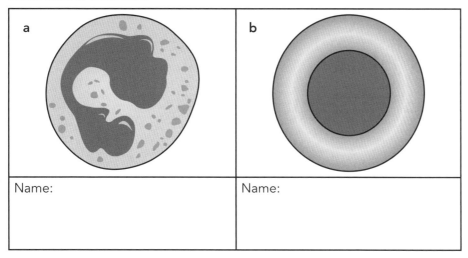

Table 7.6

Challenge

4   Name and give the function of each of the blood cells in Table 7.7.

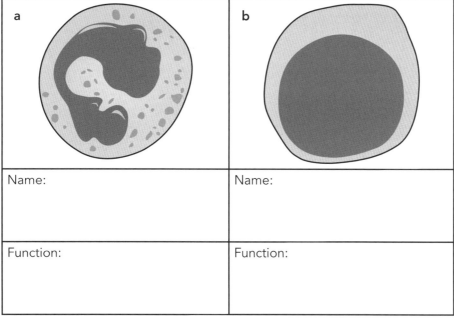

Table 7.7

Chapter 8

Diseases and immunity

> Pathogens and transmissible diseases

Exercise 8.1

IN THIS EXERCISE YOU WILL:

- check that you understand the meanings of some important words

- try to give clear descriptions of processes, in your own words

- practise constructing a bar chart

- make suggestions to explain data provided

- practise writing an answer where you are not given much help to structure it

- practise calculating a percentage increase.

KEY WORDS

transmissible disease: a disease that can be passed from one host to another; transmissible diseases are caused by pathogens.

Focus

The common cold is caused by viruses. We can get a cold if we breathe in droplets of moisture breathed out by someone else who has a cold.

1   Which word in the sentences above refers to a pathogen?

....

2   Is the common cold a transmissible disease? Explain your answer.

....

3   List *two* other types of pathogen, besides the type that causes the common cold.

i   ....

ii   ....

Practice

Table 8.1 shows the number of reported cases of food poisoning caused by five different pathogens. It also shows the percentage of these reported cases caused by each pathogen.

Pathogen	Number of cases	Percentage of cases
Norovirus	5 461 731	58
Salmonella	1 027 561	11
Clostridium	965 958	10
Campylobacter	845 024	9
Staphylococcus	241 148	3

Table 8.1

4 Explain what is meant by the term *pathogen*.

....

5 Plot the data for the percentage of cases caused by each pathogen as a bar chart.

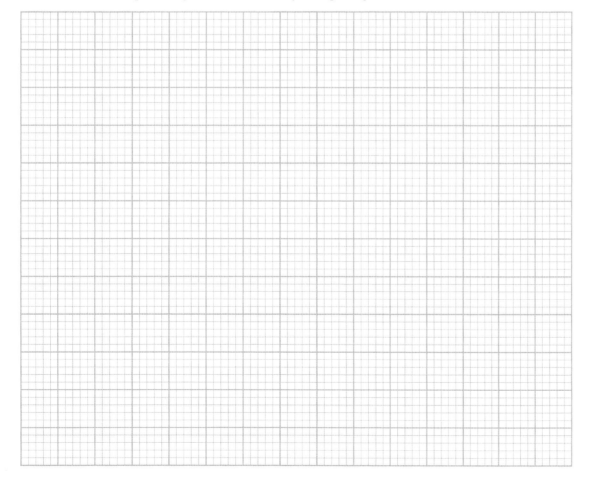

SELF ASSESSMENT

How confident do you feel about drawing bar charts? Rate yourself for each of the points in the checklist using:

☺ if you did it really well

😐 if you made a good attempt at it and partly succeeded

☹ if you did not try to do it, or did not succeed.

Checklist	Rating
The x-axis is labelled 'Pathogen'.	
The x-axis has the names of the five pathogens, equally spaced along the axis.	
The y-axis is labelled 'Percentage of cases'.	
The scale on the y-axis runs from 0 to 60.	
The scale on the y-axis goes up in sensible intervals – for example, 5 for each large square.	
The bars are all drawn accurately, using a ruler.	
All the bars are the same width.	
The bars do not touch.	

6   Suggest why the percentages of cases caused by these five pathogens do not add up to 100.

   ....

   ....

   ....

7 Suggest why the actual number of cases of food poisoning may have been much greater than the numbers shown in Table 8.1.

....

....

....

8 One type of food poisoning is caused by bacteria called *E. coli*. Suggest how *E. coli* is transmitted from an infected person to an uninfected person.

....

....

....

....

Challenge

The graph in Figure 8.1 shows information about the mass of solid waste generated in Australia in 2002–2003 and in 2006–2007, and how this waste was disposed of.

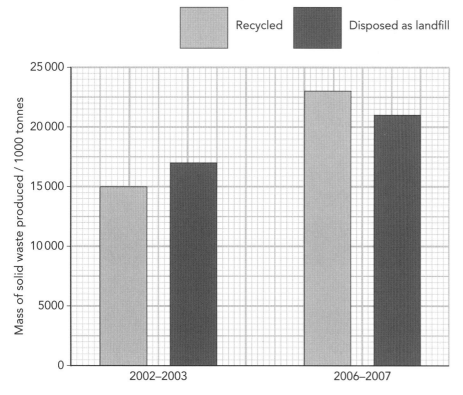

Figure 8.1: Mass of solid waste disposed of as landfill and mass recycled for two time periods in Australia.

9 Compare the data for 2006–2007 with the data for 2002–2003. (You should be able to think of at least three different comparisons to make, but see if you can make four.) Use numbers from Figure 8.1 to support your comparisons.

....

....

....

....

....

....

....

....

> **TIP**
>
> Start by thinking what you can compare and make a list. Then make notes for each comparison, remembering to try to use numbers where you can. Do not start writing your final answer until you have done this. Use comparative words in your answer – such as 'more' and 'bigger increase'.

10 Suggest the benefits of increasing the amount of waste that we recycle, rather than disposing of it in landfill sites.

....

....

....

....

....

....

....

....

11 a Calculate the total mass of waste produced in 2002–2003 and in 2006–2007 using Figure 8.1. Show your working.

Total waste in 2002–2003 ....

Total waste in 2006–2007 ....

b Calculate the increase in total waste between 2002–2003 and 2006–2007 using Figure 8.1.

....

c Use your answer to **b** to calculate the percentage increase in waste between 2002–2003 and 2006–2007, using this formula:

$$\text{percentage increase} = \frac{\text{increase in total waste}}{\text{total waste in } 2002-2003} \times 100$$

Show your working.

....

Exercise 8.2

IN THIS EXERCISE YOU WILL:

- consider how the body prevents pathogens from entering
- think of ways to prevent the spread of food poisoning
- suggest ways to reduce the spread of malaria.

Focus

1 Outline how each of these body defences helps to protect us from pathogens.

a Stomach acid

....

....

b Mucus

....

....

2   List *three* ways to avoid food poisoning at home.

   i   ....

   ii   ....

   iii ....

Practice

3   Malaria is an infectious disease. The pathogen that causes malaria is transferred
by mosquitoes. When a mosquito bites an infected person, the pathogen is
taken into the gut of the mosquito. When that mosquito bites someone else,
the pathogen can be introduced to their blood.

   Mosquitoes need access to still water, such as ponds and lakes, in order to
reproduce because they lay eggs in water.

   a   Suggest *three* ways in which individual people can protect themselves
from malaria.

      i   ....

      ii   ....

      iii ....

   b   Some countries have a large number of malaria cases every year.

      Suggest *three* ways in which governments can reduce the spread of malaria in
these countries.

      i   ....

      ii   ....

      iii ....

Challenge

4   Explain why the methods for preventing food poisoning and the methods for
preventing malaria are different.

   ....

   ....

   ....

Exercise 8.3

IN THIS EXERCISE YOU WILL:

- recall what is meant by active immunity and how it is acquired
- describe what antibodies are and how they work
- interpret information from a graph.

Focus

1   During the COVID-19 pandemic, many people gained active immunity to the pathogen.

   a   Describe what is meant by active immunity.

     ....

     ....

   b   People gained active immunity in *two* different ways. Describe what these are.

     i   ....

     ii   ....

Practice

2   **a**   Describe what antibodies are.

     ....

     ....

   b   Explain how antibodies work.

     ....

     ....

     ....

   c   Explain why antibodies to the influenza pathogen will not work against the measles pathogen.

     ....

     ....

Challenge

3 The graph in Figure 8.2 shows the quantity of antibody in a person's blood after they were infected with a pathogen.

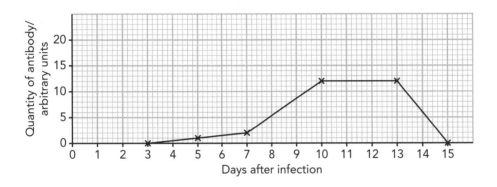

Figure 8.2: Quantity of antibody in a person's blood after they were infected with a pathogen.

The person was infected with the pathogen at day 0.

a Describe the pattern shown in Figure 8.2.

....

....

....

....

....

....

b Suggest what is happening in the immune system on days 1 and 2.

....

....

....

› The immune response

Exercise 8.4

IN THIS EXERCISE YOU WILL:

- analyse data presented in a complex graph

- think about the difference between correlation and causation

- explain how vaccines work

- apply your knowledge in a new context.

Focus

Polio (short for poliomyelitis) is a disease caused by a virus, which is transmitted from one person to another through food or water contaminated with faeces from an infected person. Many people show no symptoms when they are infected, but in a small percentage of cases the virus enters the spinal cord and causes damage to neurones that normally send nerve impulses to muscles. This results in paralysis. Polio is much more common in young children than in adults.

- The World Health Organization (WHO) is committed to eradicating polio from the world. This is being done by a vaccination programme.

- The graph in Figure 8.3 shows the estimated number of cases of polio in the world between 1980 and 2005, and the percentage of children who were vaccinated each year.

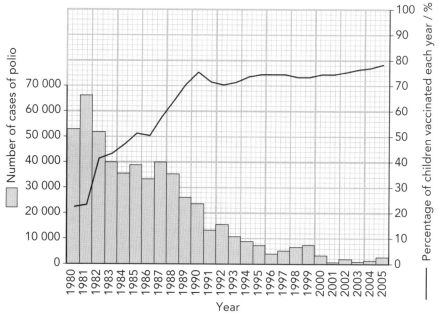

Figure 8.3: Graph showing global polio cases between 1980 and 2005, and the percentage of children vaccinated.

1 Suggest why children are more likely to get polio than adults. (You may be able to think of more than one reason.)

....

....

....

2 Describe the changes in the numbers of polio cases between 1980 and 2005 on the graph in Figure 8.3.

....

....

....

....

....

> **TIP**
>
> Remember to quote numbers from the graph in your answer.

Practice

3 Evaluate how well the data in Figure 8.3 support the conclusion that vaccination has caused a decrease in polio cases.

....

....

....

....

....

> **TIP**
>
> Remember that correlation does not always imply causation. However, we might still be able to assume causation if we can give a good explanation for it.

4 The polio vaccine is unusual, because it can be given by mouth rather than by injection. Suggest why most vaccines have to be given by injection.

....

....

....

....

....

> **TIP**
>
> Think about what happens inside the alimentary canal.

Challenge

5   The polio vaccine contains polio viruses that have been treated to make them
unable to reproduce in the body.

Explain how the polio vaccine makes a person immune to polio.

....

....

....

....

....

....

....

....

> Chapter 9

Gas exchange and respiration

> Gas exchange

Exercise 9.1

IN THIS EXERCISE YOU WILL:

- label a diagram of the breathing system
- compare the composition of inhaled and exhaled air
- explain changes in breathing rate between resting and exercising
- explain how the body uses oxygen.

KEY WORDS

alveoli: tiny air-filled sacs in the lungs where gas exchange takes place.

gas exchange: the diffusion of oxygen and carbon dioxide into and out of an organism's body.

Focus

1 Figure 9.1 is a diagram of the breathing system. Complete the figure by adding the following labels in the spaces provided.

> larynx   rib   intercostal muscle   lung   trachea
>
> diaphragm   bronchus   bronchiole   alveolus

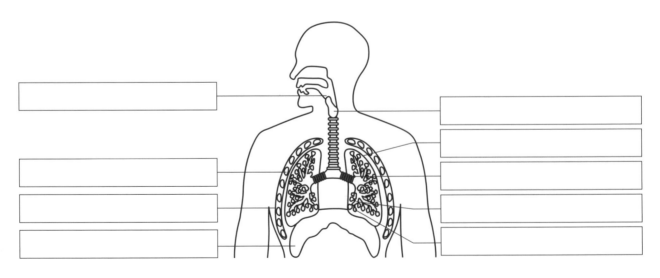

Figure 9.1: Diagram of the breathing system.

Practice

Table 9.1 shows the composition of inhaled air and exhaled air.

Gas	% in inhaled air	% in exhaled air
nitrogen	74	74
oxygen	21	16
argon	0.9	0.9
carbon dioxide	0.04	4.0

Table 9.1

2 **a** Name the gas that shows the largest change in composition between inhaled and exhaled air.

....

b Name *one* gas that does not change in composition between inhaled and exhaled air.

....

i Suggest what this implies about this gas with respect to the human body.

....

c Describe a test that proves carbon dioxide to be present in exhaled air.

....

....

....

Challenge

3 Table 9.1 shows that we take in oxygen from air.

a State what oxygen is used for in the body.

....

b Explain why the percentage of oxygen does not drop to zero in exhaled air.

....

....

....

KEY WORDS

gas exchange surface: a part of the body where gas exchange between the body and the environment takes place.

4 During exercise, our breathing rate changes compared with when we are resting. Describe the processes that occur to make this happen.

....

....

....

....

Exercise 9.2

IN THIS EXERCISE YOU WILL:

- practise handling data provided in a table, including making a calculation
- compare two sets of data
- use information provided, and your own understanding, to suggest an explanation for patterns in data.

Focus

Rat lungs have a similar structure to human lungs. Researchers measured the surface area of the alveoli in the lungs of female and male rats of different ages. They also measured the mass of each rat, and calculated the number of square centimetres of alveolar surface area per gram of body mass.

Their results are shown in Table 9.2.

Age/days	Ratio of alveolar surface area to body mass/cm² per gram	
	Females	Males
21	21.6	23.1
33	15.4	15.2
45	12.9	12.1
60	13.4	10.9
95	13.4	9.4

Table 9.2

1   Plot line graphs on the grid below to display these data. Plot both curves on the same pair of axes.

> **TIP**
>
> Take care with the scale for the x-axis.

2   A 21-day-old male rat has a body mass of 40 g.

Using the data in Table 9.2, calculate this rat's probable alveolar surface area. Show your working.

> **TIP**
>
> Look at the ratio of alveolar surface area to body mass for a 21-day-old male rat. This tells you how many cm^2 of surface there are for each gram of body mass.

....

Practice

3   Suggest why the researchers recorded the ratio of alveolar surface area to body mass, rather than just the alveolar surface area.

....

....

....

4 Compare the results for female and male rats, shown in Table 9.2.

....

....

....

....

....

....

Challenge

5 Female rats are able to become pregnant when they are about 60 days old. Their lungs then have to supply oxygen for themselves, and also for their developing offspring. Suggest how the data in Table 9.2 could relate to this fact.

....

....

....

....

....

PEER ASSESSMENT

Exchange your response with that of a partner.

Did your partner make a good suggestion to explain how the data provided in Table 9.2 support the statement?

> Respiration

Exercise 9.3

IN THIS EXERCISE YOU WILL:

- check your understanding of respiration, by correcting someone else's mistakes

- compare aerobic and anaerobic respiration

- practise constructing and completing a results table

- apply your knowledge of respiration and photosynthesis to make a prediction

- apply your knowledge of respiration to suggest explanations.

KEY WORDS

aerobic respiration: chemical reactions that take place in mitochondria, which use oxygen to break down glucose and other nutrient molecules to release energy for the cell to use.

anaerobic respiration: chemical reactions in cells that break down nutrient molecules to release energy, without using oxygen.

Focus

1 Here are some statements that a student made, about respiration. Each statement has a mistake in it.

Rewrite each statement, correcting the mistakes.

a   Every cell uses energy to help it to respire.

   ....

   ....

b   Aerobic respiration produces energy by combining nutrient molecules, such as glucose, with oxygen.

   ....

   ....

c   In human muscle, both aerobic respiration and anaerobic respiration produce carbon dioxide.

   ....

   ....

Practice

A student had a fish tank in which she kept tropical fish. She knew it was meant to be a good idea to keep living plants in the tank as well. She wanted to find out how the plants affected the concentration of carbon dioxide in the water.

Figure 9.2 shows the apparatus that she set up. She used hydrogencarbonate indicator solution because it is yellow when it contains a large amount of carbon dioxide, orange when a small amount of carbon dioxide is present and red when it contains no carbon dioxide at all.

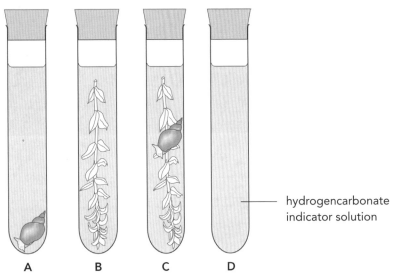

hydrogencarbonate indicator solution

A   B   C   D

Figure 9.2: A student's apparatus.

The student left all four tubes in a sunny place for 30 minutes. When she looked at the tubes again, she found the indicator had turned yellow in tube A, deep red in tube B, and stayed orange in tubes C and D.

2 Draw a results table in the space below and fill it in to show the student's results.

3 Explain the results in each tube.

Tube A

....

....

Tube B

....

....

Tube C

....

....

Tube D

....

....

TIP

Remember that all living organisms respire all the time, and that plants also photosynthesise in the light.

4 Predict the results that would be obtained if all the tubes were left in the dark.

....

....

....

....

5 Discuss what these results and your predictions in question **4** suggest about whether or not it is good to have living plants in a fish tank.

....

....

....

....

Challenge

A student is uses insects to investigate one of the characteristics of living things.
She sets up the apparatus shown in Figure 9.3.

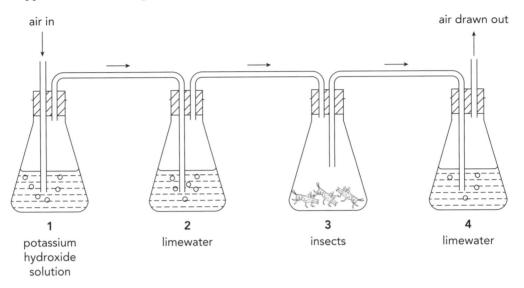

Figure 9.3: A student's apparatus.

Air is drawn through the apparatus from left to right as shown. The potassium
hydroxide in flask 1 removes any carbon dioxide from the air.

6   a   i   State the purpose of the limewater in flask 2.

....

....

ii   Predict the appearance of the limewater in flask 2 after 10 minutes.

....

....

b   i   State the purpose of the limewater in flask 4.

....

....

ii   Predict the appearance of the limewater in flask 4 after 10 minutes.

....

....

c   Suggest a control for this experiment.

....

....

d   i   State the appearance of the liquid in flask 4 at the end of the experiment
          if it had contained water and Universal (full range) Indicator rather
          than limewater.

....

....

     ii   Explain your answer to **d i**.

....

....

e   Name the process inside living cells that is responsible for the changes that are
     observed in this experiment.

....

Exercise 9.4

IN THIS EXERCISE YOU WILL:

- describe anaerobic respiration

- write an equation for anaerobic respiration

- compare anaerobic respiration with aerobic respiration

- explain what happens after vigorous exercise as a result of
  anaerobic respiration.

Focus

1   Describe what is meant by the term *anaerobic respiration*.

....

....

2 Write the word equation for anaerobic respiration in muscles.

....

Practice

3 State *three* differences between anaerobic respiration and aerobic respiration.

i anaerobic respiration ....

ii anaerobic respiration ....

iii anaerobic respiration ....

Challenge

4 During vigorous exercise, anaerobic respiration can occur in muscles.
Explain what happens in the body after such vigorous exercise, as a result of
anaerobic respiration happening.

....

....

....

....

....

....

Chapter 10

Coordination and response

> Coordination and response

Exercise 10.1

IN THIS EXERCISE YOU WILL:

- practise using the new vocabulary for this topic
- check that you understand reflex arcs
- plan an experiment, with no help.

Focus

1   Complete the sentences about the human nervous system, using words from the following list.

axon   central   chemical   electrical   neurones

peripheral   receptors   stimulus

The human nervous system is made of specialised cells called _____.

These cells have a long thread of cytoplasm called an _____.

They can transmit _____ impulses very quickly.

The brain and spinal cord make up the _____ nervous system. The nerves

outside the brain and spinal cord form the _____ nervous system.

KEY WORDS

axon: a long, thin fibre of cytoplasm that extends from the cell body of a neurone.

central nervous system (CNS): the brain and spinal cord.

motor neurone: a neurone that transmits electrical impulses from the central nervous system to an effector.

nerve impulse: an electrical signal that passes rapidly along an axon.

neurone: a cell that is specialised for conducting electrical impulses rapidly.

peripheral nervous system (PNS): the nerves outside the brain and spinal cord.

receptors: cells or groups of cells that detect stimuli.

Practice

Figure 10.1 shows a reflex arc.

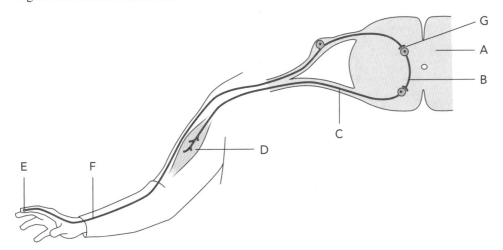

Figure 10.1: A reflex arc.

KEY WORDS

reflex action: a rapid, automatic response to a stimulus, which does not involve conscious thought.

reflex arc: a series of neurones (sensory, relay and motor) that transmit electrical impulses from a receptor to an effector.

relay neurone: a neurone that transmits electrical impulses within the central nervous system.

sensory neurone: a neurone that transmits electrical impulses from a receptor to the central nervous system.

stimuli: changes in the environment that can be detected by organisms.

2 Complete Table 10.1 to identify the labelled structures in Figure 10.1.

Letter	Name
A	
B	
C	
D	
E	
F	
G	

Table 10.1

3 On Figure 10.1, draw *one* arrow on each of parts B, C and F, to show the direction in which a nerve impulse travels.

Challenge

4 Reaction time is the time between receiving a stimulus and responding to it. Here is a method for measuring reaction time.

- Ask your partner to hold a ruler vertically, with the 0 at the bottom.

- Place your hand at the bottom of the ruler, exactly opposite the 0 mark, ready to catch it. Rest your hand on the bench, so that it cannot change its position (see Figure 10.2).

- Your partner lets go of the ruler, and you catch it as quickly as you can.

- Read off the distance on the ruler where you have caught it. The faster your reaction time, the shorter the distance.

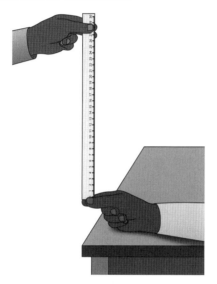

Figure 10.2: Method for measuring reaction time.

Plan an experiment to test this hypothesis:

Consuming drinks containing caffeine decreases reaction time.

....

....

....

....

....

....

....

> **TIP**
>
> It is not easy to standardise variables for this experiment. Think about how you can make a really good attempt to standardise all the variables that might affect your trust in your results.

....

....

....

....

....

....

....

> Hormones

Exercise 10.2

IN THIS EXERCISE YOU WILL:

- check that you know the vocabulary for this topic

- describe the effects of adrenaline

- compare the way that the nervous system and the endocrine (hormonal) system bring about control and coordination.

KEY WORDS

adrenaline: a hormone secreted by the adrenal glands, which prepares the body for fight or flight.

endocrine glands: glands that secrete hormones.

hormones: chemicals that are produced by a gland and carried in the blood, which alter the activities of their specific target organs.

target organs: organs whose activity is altered by a hormone.

Focus

1   Draw *one* line to match each name with its description.

Name	Description
hormone	a hormone secreted by the testes
target organ	a chemical substance produced by an endocrine gland and carried in the blood
insulin	a part of the body that is affected by a hormone
ovaries	organs that secrete oestrogen
testosterone	a hormone secreted by the pancreas

Practice

Adrenaline is secreted when we are nervous.

2   Name the glands that secrete adrenaline.

....

....

3   Outline the effects of adrenaline.

....

....

....

....

Challenge

4   Complete Table 10.2, to compare the features of control and coordination by nerves and by hormones.

Feature	Control and coordination by nerves	Control and coordination by hormones
how information is transmitted between different parts of the body		
speed of action		
duration of effect		

Table 10.2

> Homeostasis

Exercise 10.3

IN THIS EXERCISE YOU WILL:

- recall information about insulin and its functions

- interpret information presented on a graph

- explain the concept of negative feedback in relation to blood glucose concentration.

Focus

In some people, the control of blood glucose concentration does not work correctly. In type 1 diabetes, insulin is not secreted.

1 Name the gland that normally secretes insulin.

   ....

2 In what circumstances does this gland normally secrete insulin?

   ....

   ....

KEY WORDS

insulin: a hormone secreted by the pancreas, which decreases blood glucose concentration.

negative feedback: a mechanism that detects a move away from the set point, and brings about actions that take the value back towards the set point.

set point: the normal value, or range of values, for a particular parameter – for example, the normal range of blood glucose concentration, or the normal body temperature.

type 1 diabetes: a condition in which insufficient insulin is secreted by the pancreas, so that blood glucose concentration is not controlled.

Practice

The graph in Figure 10.3 shows the concentration of glucose in the blood of two people, after they had eaten a meal containing starch at time 0. One person had type 1 diabetes, and the other did not.

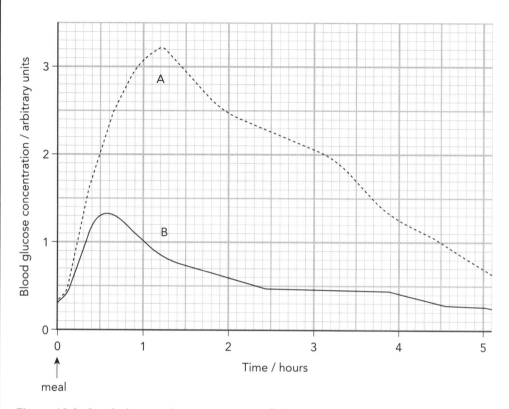

Figure 10.3: Graph showing the concentration of glucose in the blood of two people, A and B.

3   Explain why the concentration of glucose in the blood increases when a person has eaten a meal containing starch.

....

....

....

....

....

....

4 Suggest which person, A or B, has type 1 diabetes. Explain your answer fully.

....

....

....

....

....

....

....

5 Explain why it is important to keep the concentration of glucose in the blood neither too high nor too low.

....

....

....

....

....

....

....

Challenge

6 Explain how negative feedback and a set point are involved in the control of blood glucose concentration.

....

....

....

....

....

....

....

> Chapter 11
Reproduction

> Asexual and sexual reproduction
Exercise 11.1

IN THIS EXERCISE YOU WILL:

- check that you understand the differences between asexual and sexual reproduction
- describe the role of gametes in reproduction.

Focus

1 Complete Table 11.1 by putting a tick (✓) or cross (✗) into each box.

Feature	Asexual reproduction	Sexual reproduction
always only one parent		
offspring are genetically identical		
gametes are involved		
a zygote is produced		

Table 11.1

Practice

2 What are the male and female gametes in a flowering plant?

....

3 What are the male and female gametes in a mammal?

....

KEY WORDS

asexual reproduction: a process resulting in the production of genetically identical offspring from one parent.

diploid: having two complete sets of chromosomes.

gamete: a sex cell; a cell with half the normal number of chromosomes, whose nucleus fuses with the nucleus of another gamete during sexual reproduction.

haploid: having only a single set of chromosomes.

sexual reproduction: a process involving the fusion of two gametes to form a zygote and the production of offspring that are genetically different from each other.

zygote: a cell that is formed by the fusion of two gametes.

4 Figure 11.1 shows a plant reproducing.

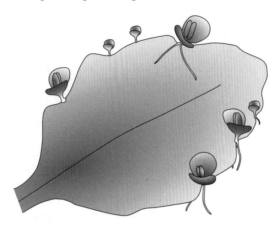

Figure 11.1: A plant reproducing.

Explain why this is an example of asexual reproduction.

....

....

....

Challenge

5 The plant shown in Figure 11.1 can also reproduce sexually.

Discuss the advantages and disadvantages of asexual and sexual reproduction to this plant in the wild.

....

....

....

....

....

6 a Explain why the nuclei of gametes must be haploid.

....

....

....

....

b   The gametes of the domestic cat each have 19 chromosomes. Write down the number of chromosomes in the zygote of a domestic cat.

....

7   A horse has 64 chromosomes and a donkey has 62 chromosomes.

a   Write down the number of chromosomes in:

a horse gamete ....

a donkey gamete. ....

b   A horse and a donkey can reproduce together sexually to produce offspring called a mule.

Write down the number of chromosomes in a mule. ....

c   Mules are classed as sterile because they cannot reproduce with each other.

Suggest why not.

....

....

....

› Sexual reproduction in plants
Exercise 11.2

IN THIS EXERCISE YOU WILL:

- practise making the kind of drawing that is used in biology
- bring together information from different topics
- apply your knowledge and understanding in an unfamiliar context.

Read the information about coffee trees.

Coffee trees are grown to produce their seeds, called coffee beans, which are used all over the world to make coffee drinks and other products. Two species of coffee tree are grown for the commercial production of coffee – *Coffea arabica* and *Coffea canephora*.

Coffee trees normally reproduce by producing seeds. They have flowers with white petals and a very pleasant scent.

KEY WORDS

anther: the structure at the top of a stamen, inside which pollen grains are made.

fertilisation: the fusion of the nuclei of two gametes.

petals: coloured structures that attract insects or birds to a flower.

Growers can also produce new coffee trees by taking cuttings. This involves cutting a piece from a stem and placing the lower end in soil. This will then grow roots and eventually grow into a new tree.

Focus

Biologists often need to describe clearly what they observe when studying organisms. One of the best ways to do this is to make a drawing.

A biological drawing needs to be simple, but clear. Sometimes, you need to label your drawing to indicate important features.

Here are some points to think about when you draw.

- Make good use of the space on your sheet of paper – your drawing should be large. However, do leave space around it so that you have room for labels.
- Always use a sharp HB pencil and have a good eraser with you.
- Keep all lines single and clear, with no breaks.
- Do not use shading.
- Do not use colours.
- Take time to get the outline of your drawing correct first, showing the correct proportions. Do this lightly to start with, so that you can rub out and try again.

Here are some points to bear in mind when you label a diagram.

- Use a ruler to draw each label line.
- Make sure the end of the label line touches the structure being labelled.
- Write the labels horizontally.
- Keep the labels well away from the edges of your drawing.
- Do not let label lines cross one another.

Figure 11.2 shows two drawings of a coffee tree flower made by learners.

KEY WORDS
pollen grains: small structures which contain the male gametes of a flower.
pollination: the transfer of pollen grains from the male part of the plant (anther of stamen) to the female part of the plant (stigma).
stigma: the part of a flower that receives pollen.

a
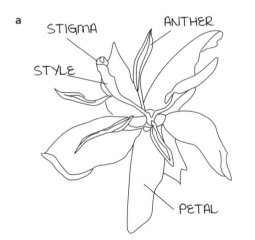

b
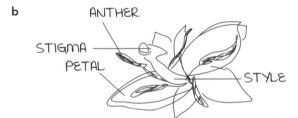

Figure 11.2 a and b: Two drawings of a coffee tree flower made by learners.

1 List *five* ways in which the first drawing (Figure 11.2a) is better than the second drawing (Figure 11.2b).

....

....

....

Practice

2 Outline the events that must happen in a flower of *Coffea arabica* before fertilisation can take place.

....

....

....

Challenge

3 Imagine that you are a coffee grower. A fungal disease called coffee rust has recently begun to attack some of your *Coffea arabica* trees. Some of them seem to be resistant to the fungus and survive, while others are badly damaged. The trees also vary in the quality of the coffee beans that they produce.

Use your understanding of the advantages and disadvantages of different methods of reproduction to suggest ways in which you might be able to produce a large number of coffee trees that are able to survive attack by coffee rust.

....

....

....

....

PEER ASSESSMENT

Exchange your answer with a partner.

Compare your ideas.

Which ideas have you both thought of? Are there any ideas that your partner thought of, but that you did not?

Give feedback to your partner. Tell them two things that they have done well, and *one* thing that could be improved.

Exercise 11.3

IN THIS EXERCISE YOU WILL:

- describe structural adaptations of wind-pollinated flowers
- consider the advantages of wind pollination.

Focus

1   Wind-pollinated flowers usually have smaller petals than insect-pollinated flowers. Also, these petals often lack the bright colours seen in insect-pollinated flowers.

Describe *two* other differences between the structures of a wind-pollinated flower and an insect-pollinated flower.

i   ....

....

ii   ....

....

Practice

2   The flowers of wind-pollinated plants can produce over 10 000 pollen grains.

The flowers of insect-pollinated plants usually produce fewer than 1000 pollen grains.

Suggest a reason for this difference.

....

....

....

Challenge

3   In 1999 some pollen grains were found in Ontario, Canada. They were confirmed to have come from a plant in Texas, USA. These pollen grains had been carried 2400 km by wind.

a   Pollen grains that are adapted to be carried by wind are small and smooth.

Suggest *one* other adaptation that differs from pollen that is carried by insects.

....

b   Travelling a longer distance is one advantage of pollen being carried by wind compared with being carried by insects.

Suggest *two* other advantages.

i   ....

....

ii ....

....

TIP

When you are asked to make suggestions, think about what you already know. Here, consider benefits to the plant of producing pollen that does not require insects for distribution.

> Sexual reproduction in humans

Exercise 11.4

IN THIS EXERCISE YOU WILL:

- check that you understand how the structures of egg and sperm cells are related to their functions

- bring together knowledge from several areas of the syllabus to make suggestions.

KEY WORDS

acrosome: a structure containing digestive enzymes, in the head of a sperm cell.

flagellum (plural flagella): a long, whip-like 'tail' structure found on sperm cells, used for swimming.

Focus

Figure 11.3 shows diagrams of human female and male gametes.

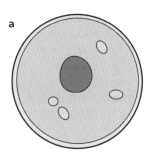

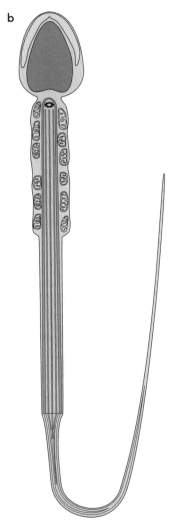

Figure 11.3 a: Human female gamete. **b:** Human male gamete.

1   Use black or blue to label all the structures on each gamete in Figure 11.3 that you would find in any animal cell.

Practice

2   Use red or another contrasting colour to label all the structures on Figure 11.3 on each gamete that are adaptations for their specialised functions. Explain how each feature that you label helps the cell to perform its function.

Challenge

3 Explain the role of enzymes in the fertilisation of a human egg by a human sperm.

....

....

....

Exercise 11.5

IN THIS EXERCISE YOU WILL:

- label diagrams of the male and female reproductive systems
- identify some parts of the reproductive systems from their functions.

Focus

1 Figure 11.4 shows the male and female reproductive systems.

Complete both diagrams by adding labels in the spaces provided.

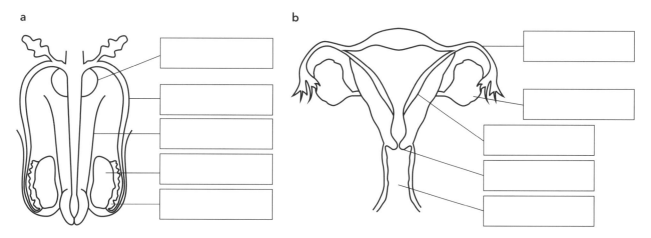

Figure 11.4 a: Human male reproductive system. **b:** Human female reproductive system.

Practice

2   Name the part of the female reproductive system

    a   where fertilisation takes place

    ....

    b   where sperm are introduced.

    ....

Challenge

3   Name the part of the male reproductive system

    a   where semen is produced

    ....

    b   that can transfer either urine or sperm.

    ....

Exercise 11.6

IN THIS EXERCISE YOU WILL:

- recall the names of male and female sex hormones
- describe the effects of these hormones at puberty
- interpret a diagram of the menstrual cycle.

Focus

1   Development of secondary sexual characteristics in boys occurs at puberty.

    a   Name the hormone that causes these changes.

    ....

    b   One example of these changes is deepening of the voice.

    Describe *two* other changes that happen in boys during puberty.

      i   ....

      ii   ....

2 Development of secondary sexual characteristics in girls also occurs at puberty.

    a Name the hormone that causes these changes.

    ....

    b One example of these changes is widening of the hips.

       Describe *two* other changes that happen in girls during puberty.

       i ....

       ii ....

Practice

3 Figure 11.5 shows how the thickness of the uterus wall changes during the 28 days of the menstrual cycle.

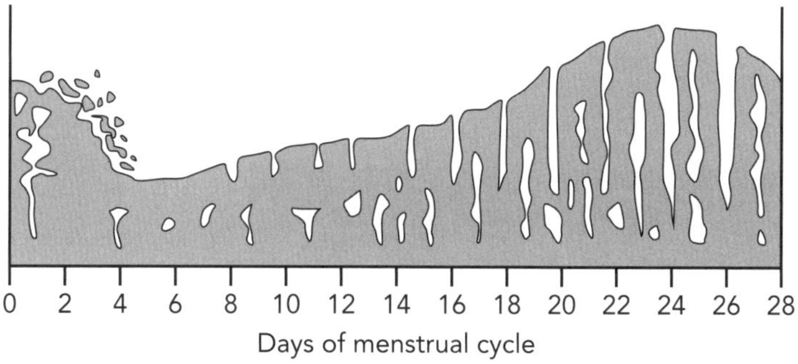

Days of menstrual cycle

Figure 11.5: How the thickness of the uterus wall changes during the menstrual cycle.

    a Use Figure 11.5 to state when menstruation occurs.

       From day _____ until day _____.

    b Use the diagram to estimate the percentage change in thickness of the uterus wall from its thinnest to its thickest.

       .... %

> **TIP**
>
> To calculate the percentage change in two values, find the difference between them and then divide this value by the value at the start. Do not forget to multiply the value you find by 100.

    c Explain why the uterus wall thickens and develops many blood vessels between days 5 and 24.

       ....

       ....

       ....

       ....

Challenge

4   One method of contraception, which can be used to minimise the chance of pregnancy, is by taking medicinal pills that contain hormones. Suggest reasons to explain how these hormones could prevent pregnancy from occurring.

....

....

....

....

....

> Sexually transmitted infections

Exercise 11.7

IN THIS EXERCISE YOU WILL:

- identify changes in the number of people infected with HIV from a graph
- make suggestions to explain unfamiliar data.

KEY WORDS

HIV/AIDS: an infectious disease caused by the viral pathogen human immunodeficiency virus (HIV), which is transmitted through the sexual and blood-to-blood contact routes and can cause weakening of the immune system, leaving patients susceptible to other diseases.

The graph in Figure 11.6 shows the number of people in the Caribbean who were known to be infected with HIV, who had AIDS and who died from AIDS, between 1982 and 2008.

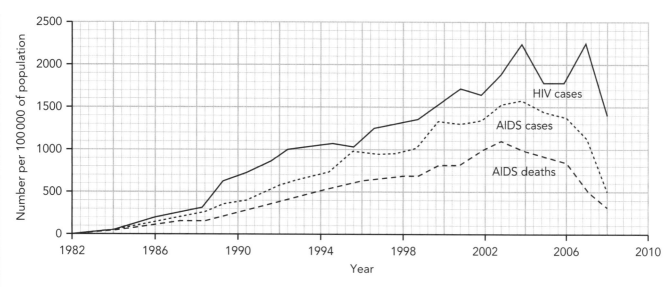

Figure 11.6: AIDS cases in the Caribbean between 1982 and 2008.

Focus

1 With reference to Figure 11.6, describe the changes in the number of people infected with HIV between 1982 and 2008.

....

....

Practice

2 Suggest why the actual number of people infected with HIV may have been greater than the numbers shown on Figure 11.6.

....

....

Challenge

3 Suggest reasons for the shape of the graphs between 2004 and 2008 in Figure 11.6.

....

....

....

....

Chapter 12
Inheritance

> Chromosomes and genes

Exercise 12.1

IN THIS EXERCISE YOU WILL:

- review your understanding of chromosomes, genes and alleles
- draw a diagram to show how sex is determined in humans
- work out the number of chromosomes in different types of cell.

KEY WORD

gene: a length of DNA that codes for one protein.

Focus

Figure 12.1 shows a chromosome, just before the cell it is part of divides.

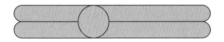

Figure 12.1: A chromosome just before cell division.

1   State the part of a cell in which chromosomes are found.

   ....

2   Name the chemical substance that contains genetic information and that is found in chromosomes.

   ....

3   Chromosomes contain genes. What is a gene?

   ....

   ....

Practice

4 Describe what is meant by the term *alleles*.

....

5 Complete this genetic diagram to show how sex is determined in humans.

genotype of father: _____; genotype of mother: _____

gametes from father: _____; gametes from mother: _____

	Father	
Mother		

genotypes of children: _____, _____, _____, _____

sex of children: _____, _____, _____, _____

Challenge

Sheep have 26 pairs of chromosomes plus one pair of sex chromosomes.

6 A sheep skin cell has a diploid nucleus and a sheep sperm cell has a haploid nucleus.

State the number of chromosomes in:

a a sheep skin cell ....

b a sheep sperm cell ....

7 State the general term given to a cell from a mammal that has a haploid nucleus.

....

> Cell division

Exercise 12.2

IN THIS EXERCISE YOU WILL:

- describe the roles of different types of cell division in multicellular organisms

- check that you understand the differences between mitosis and meiosis.

Focus

Use words from the following list to complete these sentences about cell division.

You can use each word once, more than once or not at all.

halved	diploid	divided	the same	replicated	starts

different	ends	stops	haploid

1   All of the chromosomes in a cell are _____ just before mitosis

_____ .

2   Cells produced by mitosis have _____ number of chromosomes as the parent cell.

3   The cells produced by mitosis each have a _____ nucleus.

Practice

Cell M is a cell in the body of an animal. It contains two sets of chromosomes. Each set is made up of 12 chromosomes.

4   a   What is the term for a cell that contains two complete sets of chromosomes?

....

b   How many chromosomes will be present in a gamete produced by this animal?

....

5   The cell divides by mitosis to produce cells P and Q.

a   How many chromosomes are there in cell P?

....

KEY WORDS

meiosis: division of a diploid nucleus, resulting in four genetically different haploid nuclei; this is sometimes called a reduction division.

mitosis: division of a cell nucleus, resulting in two genetically identical nuclei (that is, with the same number and kinds of chromosomes as the parent nucleus).

b Are cells P and Q genetically different, or genetically identical to the parent cell?

....

c List *three* roles of mitosis in plants and animals.

i ....

ii ....

iii ....

Challenge

6 Cell M now divides by meiosis.

Outline *three* differences between the outcome of this division, and the division by mitosis described in question **5**.

> **TIP**
>
> When you are asked to outline differences, you can do this in the form of a table if you find it easier than writing sentences.

i ....

ii ....

iii ....

> Monohybrid inheritance
Exercise 12.3

IN THIS EXERCISE YOU WILL:

• check your recall of the key words used in genetics.

Focus

1 Distinguish between each of these terms:

a Homozygous and heterozygous

....

....

....

b Genotype and phenotype.

....

....

....

....

Practice

2 Distinguish between each of these terms:

a Gene and allele

....

....

....

....

b Dominant and recessive.

....

....

Challenge

3 Write a definition for the term *pure breeding*, using as many as possible of the key terms you have encountered in this exercise as possible.

....

....

....

....

KEY WORDS

alleles: alternative forms of a gene.

dominant allele: an allele that is expressed if it is present (e.g. **G**).

genetic diagram: a standard way of showing all the steps in making predictions about the probable genotypes and phenotypes of the offspring from two parents.

genotype: the genetic makeup of an organism in terms of the alleles present (e.g. **GG**).

heterozygous: having two different alleles of a particular gene (e.g. **Gg**).

homozygous: having two identical alleles of a particular gene (e.g. **GG** or **gg**).

phenotype: the observable features of an organism.

recessive allele: an allele that is only expressed when there is no dominant allele of the gene present (e.g. **g**).

Exercise 12.4

IN THIS EXERCISE YOU WILL:

- distinguish between genotype and phenotype

- practise using a genetic diagram

- practise using a pedigree diagram to work out genotypes

- practise explaining your deductions clearly and logically.

Focus

Fruit flies are often used for research into genetics. Figure 12.2 shows a fruit fly.

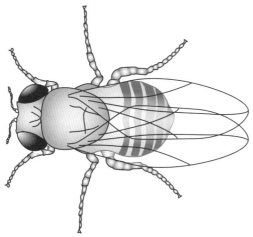

Figure 12.2: A fruit fly, *Drosophila melanogaster*.

1 Fruit flies can have normal wings or vestigial (really small) wings. The allele for normal wings, **N**, is dominant. The allele for vestigial wings, **n**, is recessive.

Complete Table 12.1 to show the possible genotypes and phenotypes for fruit fly wings. Be very careful to write the letters **N** and **n** so that there is no doubt whether each one is a capital letter or a small letter.

Genotype	Phenotype

Table 12.1

Practice

2   Complete the genetic diagram to predict the genotypes and phenotypes of the
    offspring of a heterozygous normal-winged fly and a vestigial-winged fly.

Parents' phenotypes   normal wings   vestigial wings

Parents' genotypes   ....

Gametes

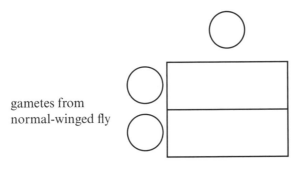

gametes from
vestigial-winged fly

gametes from
normal-winged fly

3   The two flies had 82 offspring.

    Predict approximately how many of these would have vestigial wings.

    ....

    ....

Challenge

The family tree (pedigree) in Figure 12.3 shows the incidence of a genetic disease called PKU in four generations of a family.

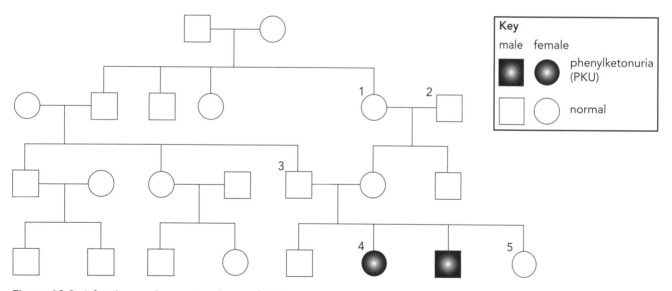

Figure 12.3: A family tree showing incidence of PKU.

4 Describe *one* piece of evidence from the diagram that suggests PKU is caused by a recessive allele.

....

....

....

5 If PKU is caused by a recessive allele, explain why it is unlikely that this allele first appeared in person 4.

....

....

....

6 In the space below, deduce the possible genotypes of persons 1, 2, 3 and 4.
Use the symbol **q** for the PKU allele and the symbol **Q** for the normal allele.

....

....

....

7 Person 5 is worried that her children might have PKU. She talks to a genetic counsellor. What might she be told?

....

....

....

....

....

Chapter 13

Variation and selection

> Variation

Exercise 13.1

IN THIS EXERCISE YOU WILL:

- recognise different types of variation
- interpret information from a histogram (frequency diagram)
- recall the cause of genetic variation.

KEY WORDS

continuous variation: variation in which there is a continuous range of phenotypes between two extremes.

discontinuous variation: variation in which there are distinct categories of phenotype, with no intermediates.

Focus

1   A person is shopping online for a new pair of gloves. The gloves are available in four sizes: small, medium, large and extra-large.

State and explain the type of variation shown by:

a   the size of people's hands

type of variation ....

explanation ....

....

b   the size of the gloves.

type of variation ....

explanation ....

....

Practice

2   Hand span is the distance from the end of the thumb to the end of the fourth finger when the hand is stretched out as shown in Figure 13.1a.

A group of students measured the hand span of their right hands. The results are shown in the histogram (frequency diagram) in Figure 13.1b.

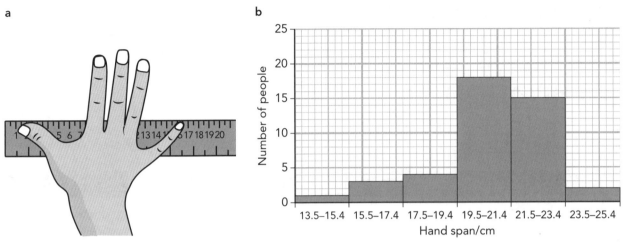

Figure 13.1 a: Measuring hand span. **b:** Histogram showing students' results.

Use the information in the histogram in Figure 13.1b to answer these questions.

a State the type of variation shown by hand span.

....

b Write down the number of people who had a hand span in the range 17.5–19.4 cm.

....

c What range of hand span included the most people?

....

d What was the total number of hand spans measured in this investigation?

....

Challenge

3 Suggest why only the right hand span was measured in this investigation. Give *two* reasons.

i ....

....

ii ....

....

〉 Selection

Exercise 13.2

IN THIS EXERCISE YOU WILL:

- check how well you understand the process of natural selection and that you can use suitable terms to describe it
- practise comparing two sets of information shown in a graph
- apply your understanding of selective breeding to a new situation
- practise describing the information shown in a graph.

KEY WORDS

adaptation: the process, resulting from natural selection, by which populations become more suited to their environment over many generations.

selection pressure: something in the environment that affects the chance that individuals with different features will survive and reproduce.

selective breeding: choosing particular organisms with desired characteristics to breed together, and continuing this over many generations.

Focus

1 Choose the best words from the following list to complete the sentences about natural selection.

alleles   community   compete   environment   fewer   generation

individuals   more   reproduce   species   survive   variation

Natural selection depends on the fact that there is _____

within populations.

In most populations, far _____ young are produced than will live long

enough to be able to _____ .

The organisms in the population have to _____ for scarce resources.

As a result, only the _____ that are best adapted to their _____

are likely to have offspring.

Their _____ are the ones that are most likely to be passed on to the next

_____ .

Practice

In the second half of the 20th century, a group of cows was put into a selective breeding programme to try to increase the milk yield over several generations. A control group was also used, in which selective breeding was not carried out.

The graph in Figure 13.2 shows the changes in milk yield over a 25-year period. The values plotted show the mean milk yield of all the cows born in a particular year.

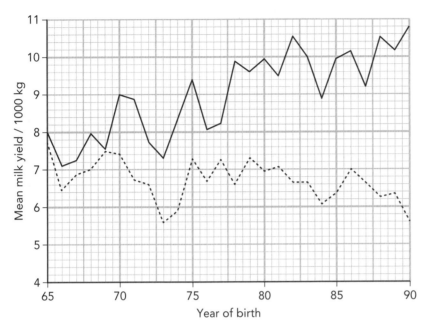

Figure 13.2: Graph showing the changes in milk yield over a 25-year period.

2 Compare the change in milk yield for the population of cows selected for milk yield with that of the control population.

....

....

....

....

....

....

....

....

....

....

3 Suggest explanations for the differences that you described in your answer to question **2**.

....

....

....

TIP
It would be good to plan your answer before you begin to write. Make a list of the points you would like to make – for example, the general trends, any particular years that stand out, data quotes for particular years, and a calculation such as the difference between the two populations in one year or the overall changes for the two populations.

....

....

....

....

....

....

....

....

Challenge

Cotton is a crop that is grown to produce fibres to make cloth. Cotton bollworms are insect pests of cotton plants. Growers use insecticides to try to reduce their losses from these pests.

The graph in Figure 13.3 shows the frequency of resistance of cotton bollworms to an insecticide that was commonly used in Australia, between 1997 and 2002.

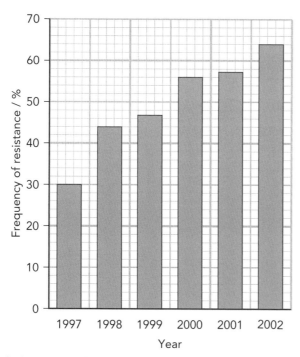

Figure 13.3: Graph showing the frequency of resistance of cotton bollworms to an insecticide.

4 Insecticides are chemical substances that kill insects. Using your knowledge of the development of resistance to antibiotics in bacteria, explain how the development of resistance to insecticides could occur.

....

....

....

....

....

....

....

....

> Drugs
Exercise 13.3

IN THIS EXERCISE YOU WILL:

- describe the meaning of the term 'drug'
- suggest why different types of drug affect different types of organism
- apply your understanding of the development of antibiotic resistance in bacteria to a new situation.

KEY WORDS

antibiotic: a chemical that kills bacteria.

insecticide: a chemical that kills insects.

Antibiotics and insecticides are both examples of drugs.

Focus

1 Describe what is meant by the term *drug*.

....

....

2   The COVID-19 pandemic was caused by a virus. Explain why doctors did not use antibiotics to treat people infected with the COVID-19 virus.

....

....

Practice

3   Using your knowledge of the development of resistance to antibiotics in bacteria, explain how the development of resistance to insecticides could occur.

....

....

....

....

....

....

....

....

....

....

....

....

PEER ASSESSMENT

Exchange your answer to Question 3 with a partner.

Give them a mark for each of the points in the checklist. Award:

2 marks if they did it really well

1 mark if they made a good attempt at it and partly succeeded

0 marks if they did not try to do it, or did not succeed.

Checklist	Marks
They have used the word 'mutation', and made clear that this happens randomly.	
They have explained how an allele for resistance to the insecticide gives a selective advantage.	
They have explained how possessing this allele affects the chances of survival and reproduction.	
They have explained how this results in more insects possessing this allele in future generations.	
Total (out of 8):	

Give feedback to your partner. Tell them *two* things that they have done well, and *one* thing that could be improved.

4   In 2017, it was estimated that more than 93 000 tonnes of antibiotics were used globally in that year. Most of these antibiotics were used in farming, where antibiotics are routinely given to many farm animals, whether or not they have an infection.

   a   Suggest how using antibiotics in this way contributes to antibiotic resistance in bacteria.

   ....

   ....

   ....

   ....

b   In 2017, it was also estimated that antibiotic use would continue to increase by all countries and rise by 12% between 2017 and 2030.

   Calculate the mass of antibiotics, in tonnes, that was predicted to be used in 2030. Show your working.

   ....

c   In the same year, it was estimated that 2 000 000 tonnes of insecticide were used.

   Suggest *two* reasons for the difference in quantity of the two substances.

   i   ....

   ....

   ii ....

   ....

Challenge

5   Suggest reasons to explain why antibiotics kill bacteria but have no effect on insects, and insecticides kill insects but have no effect on bacteria.

   ....

   ....

   ....

   ....

Chapter 14
Organisms and their environment

> Energy flow

Exercise 14.1

IN THIS EXERCISE YOU WILL:

- describe feeding relationships
- identify trophic levels
- carry out a calculation on energy transfer.

Focus

1   What is the term used to describe all of the organisms, belonging to all the different species, that live in a particular area?

   ....

2   What is the term used to describe all of the feeding relationships between the organisms that live in an area?

   ....

3   Where does the energy come from to sustain all of the organisms in the area?

   ....

Practice

4   Figure 14.1 shows the energy contained in four trophic levels of a food chain. The numbers are in units of energy.

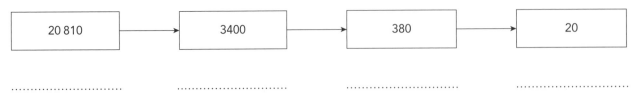

   ....

Figure 14.1: The energy contained in four trophic levels of a food chain.

a Explain what is meant by the term *trophic level*.

....

....

b Describe what the arrows represent.

....

c Underneath each box in Figure 14.1, write the correct term for the organisms in that trophic level.

Challenge

5 **a** Calculate the percentage of energy in the first trophic level that is transferred to the fourth trophic level. Show your working.

....

b Describe where the rest of the energy goes.

....

....

....

> Food chains and food webs

Exercise 14.2

IN THIS EXERCISE YOU WILL:

- use information to construct a food web

- identify trophic levels

- carry out a calculation

- interpret information from a food web.

Focus

In a field, grass and other plants grow. Mice and voles eat the seeds of all the plants. Grasshoppers eat the grass leaves. Spiders eat grasshoppers. The mice are eaten by snakes and foxes. Spiders are eaten by small birds.

1   In the space below, construct a food web to show the feeding relationships in the field.

SELF ASSESSMENT

How easy did you find it to construct the food web? Is there anything you would change if you did it again?

....

....

....

Practice

Use the food web shown in Figure 14.2 to answer questions **2–5**.

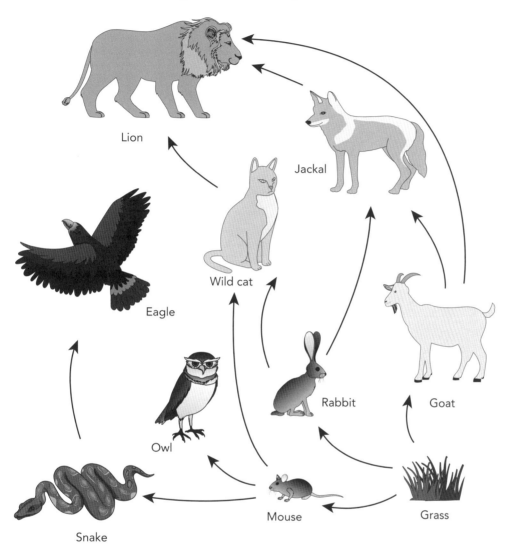

Figure 14.2: An example of a food web from an ecosystem in Africa.

2   How many trophic levels are shown?

   ....

3   How many primary consumers are shown?

   ....

4　From the organisms shown, name:

a　one herbivore

....

b　one carnivore.

....

Challenge

5　**a**　Name *one* organism in Figure 14.2 that occupies more than one trophic level.

....

b　Suggest *two* advantages to this organism of occupying more than one trophic level.

i　...

....

ii　...

....

6　Goats are one example of an animal that can be farmed for human food. We can get meat and milk from them.

Some people are suggesting that one way to sustain a growing human population is to encourage more people to eat vegetarian diets. Explain this reasoning.

....

....

....

....

TIP
Consider what you know about energy losses in food chains when you come to answer this question. If humans eat a diet that is more vegetarian, why would there be more food available for other people?

> Carbon cycle

Exercise 14.3

IN THIS EXERCISE YOU WILL:

- use a diagram to make conclusions
- use your understanding to make predictions.

KEY WORDS

decomposer: an organism that gets its energy from dead or waste organic matter.

fossil fuel: a non-renewable substance that can be burned to release energy.

Figure 14.3 shows how carbon circulates through an ecosystem.

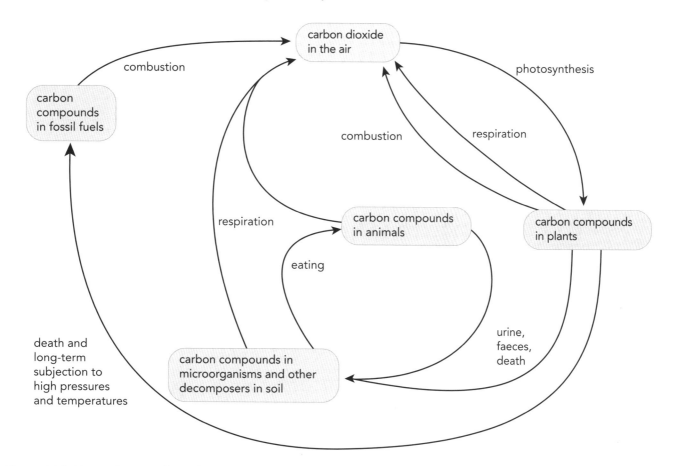

Figure 14.3: How carbon circulates through an ecosystem.

Focus

1   State the name of the only process shown in Figure 14.3 that removes carbon dioxide from the air.

   ....

Practice

2   State *two* carbon compounds that are found in the body tissues of animals.

   ....

Challenge

3   Explain what will happen to the quantity of carbon dioxide in the air if fossil fuels are burned faster than they are formed.

   ....

   ....

Chapter 15

Human influences on ecosystems

> Habitat destruction

Exercise 15.1

IN THIS EXERCISE YOU WILL:

- use your understanding of natural selection and habitats to make suggestions

- look carefully at a set of data, and then use this and your own understanding to make predictions.

KEY WORD
habitat: the place where an organism lives.

New Zealand has been separated from the other land masses on Earth for millions of years. Fossils show that very few land-living mammals ever evolved there, but birds and bats were able to colonise. Until humans arrived there were no predatory animals, and the native birds have not evolved adaptations that would help them to avoid predation. Humans probably first arrived in New Zealand about 1500 years ago. Unintentionally, they brought rats with them, and since then have introduced other mammals. This has affected the native species.

Focus

1 Suggest why birds and bats, but not other mammals, were able to colonise New Zealand.

....

....

Practice

2 In 2001, New Zealand had a total area of 11.3 Mha (megahectares) of forest. Between 2001 and 2021, this area of forest was decreased by 12%.

   a Calculate the area of forest that was lost between 2001 and 2021 in New Zealand. Show your working.

....

b Suggest *three* reasons for this change in area of forest.

i ....

ii ....

iii ....

c Studies of bird populations in New Zealand have shown that the numbers of some bird species have dropped significantly because of the loss of forest.

Give *three* reasons why loss of forest causes bird populations to fall.

i ....

ii ....

iii ....

Challenge

3 Use the theory of natural selection to suggest why many New Zealand birds are not able to fly. (This is quite a tricky question. You will need to think about selection pressures, and the costs to a bird of being able to fly.)

....

....

....

....

....

....

....

....

....

....

....

....

4   Introduced animals can also harm populations of native plants.
Nikau palms are found only in New Zealand and its surrounding islands,
such as Great Barrier Island.

Researchers counted the numbers of Nikau palm seedlings in areas where rats
have been trapped and removed, and in areas where no trapping was done.
The results are shown in Figure 15.1.

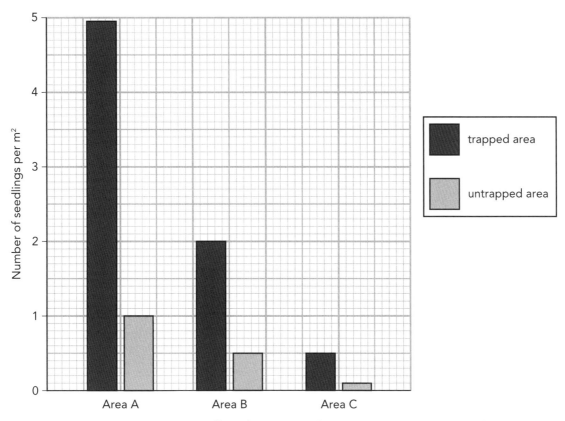

Figure 15.1: An investigation into the effect of trapping and removing rats on the number of Nikau palm seedlings.

Use the data in Figure 15.1 to suggest how removing rats could affect the
population of Nikau palms on Great Barrier Island.

....

....

....

....

> Conservation

Exercise 15.2

IN THIS EXERCISE YOU WILL:

- apply your understanding of threats to endangered species in a new context.

KEY WORDS

endangered species: species that are found in very low numbers, which means that they are at risk of extinction.

extinction: the process that leads to the complete absence of a species.

Focus

Table 15.1 lists four species of mammal in Chile that were considered to be endangered in 1983. It also shows the reasons why each mammal was endangered.

Species	Description of species	Main reason why it is endangered	Other reason why it is endangered
Pudu puda	small deer	loss of habitat	hunting; diseases transferred from introduced species
Ctenomys robustus	burrowing rodent	loss of habitat	
Chinchilla lanigera	burrowing rodent	hunting	loss of habitat
Lutra provocax	otter	hunting	

Table 15.1

1   What is meant by the term *species*?

   ....

   ....

2   State what is meant by an endangered species.

   ....

   ....

3   Outline *two* reasons why the habitat of a species may be lost.

i   ....

ii   ....

Practice

4   Explain why loss of habitat can cause a species to become endangered.

....

....

....

....

5   *Chinchilla lanigera* and *Lutra provocax* are now protected and are no longer hunted. Despite this, both species are still endangered.

Use the information in Table 15.1 to suggest why, despite the ban on hunting, *C. lanigera* is still endangered.

....

....

....

....

6   Explain how captive breeding programmes could help the populations of *Chinchilla lanigera* and *Lutra provocax* to recover.

....

....

....

....

Challenge

7 Introduced animals may carry pathogens which do not threaten them but can be very harmful to native species.

Use your knowledge of the immune response to suggest why animals such as *Pudu puda* may be harmed by diseases transferred from introduced species.

....

....

....

....

....

....

> TIP
>
> Remember that there may be more than one suitable answer for a 'suggest' question. You need to think about how you can use your knowledge and understanding to provide a good answer to the question.

PEER ASSESSMENT

Exchange your answer to question **7** with a partner.

How easy is it to understand the answer they have written?

Are their suggestions the same as yours?

Have they made any good suggestions that you did not think of?

Give feedback to your partner. Tell them *two* things that they have done well, and *one* thing that they could improve.

⟩ Glossary

absorption: the movement of nutrients from the alimentary canal into the blood.

acrosome: a structure containing digestive enzymes, in the head of a sperm cell.

active immunity: long-term defence against a pathogen by antibody production in the body.

active site: the part of an enzyme molecule to which the substrate temporarily binds.

active transport: the movement of molecules or ions through a cell membrane from a region of lower concentration to a region of higher concentration (i.e. against a concentration gradient) using energy from respiration.

adaptation: the process, resulting from natural selection, by which populations become more suited to their environment over many generations.

adrenaline: a hormone secreted by the adrenal glands, which prepares the body for fight or flight.

aerobic respiration: a chemical reaction that happens in mitochondria, where oxygen is used to release energy from glucose.

alleles: alternative forms of a gene.

alveoli: tiny air-filled sacs in the lungs where gas exchange takes place.

amino acids: substances with molecules containing carbon, hydrogen, oxygen and nitrogen; there are 20 different amino acids found in organisms.

anaerobic respiration: chemical reactions in cells that break down nutrient molecules to release energy, without using oxygen.

anther: the structure at the top of a stamen, inside which pollen grains are made.

antibiotic: a chemical that kills bacteria.

antibodies: proteins secreted by white blood cells, which bind to pathogens and help to destroy them.

antigen: a chemical that is recognised by the body as being 'foreign' – that is, it is not part of the body's normal set of chemical substances – and stimulates the production of antibodies.

aorta: the largest artery in the body, which receives oxygenated blood from the left ventricle and delivers it to the body organs.

arbitrary units: sometimes used on a graph scale to represent quantitative differences between values, instead of 'real' units such as seconds or centimetres; this is usually because the real units would be very complicated to use.

asexual reproduction: a process resulting in the production of genetically identical offspring from one parent.

atria: the thin-walled chambers at the top of the heart, which receive blood.

axon: a long, thin fibre of cytoplasm that extends from the cell body of a neurone.

bacteria: unicellular organisms whose cells do not contain a nucleus.

balanced diet: a diet that contains all of the required nutrients, in suitable proportions, and the right amount of energy.

Benedict's solution: a blue liquid that turns orange-red when heated with reducing sugar.

bile: an alkaline fluid produced by the liver, which helps with fat digestion.

bile duct: the tube that carries bile from the gall bladder to the duodenum.

biuret reagent: a blue solution that turns purple when mixed with amino acids or proteins.

carbohydrates: substances that include sugars, starch and cellulose; they contain carbon, hydrogen and oxygen.

cell: the smallest unit from which all organisms are made.

cell membrane: a very thin layer surrounding the cytoplasm of every cell; it controls what enters and leaves the cell.

cell sap: the fluid that fills the large vacuoles in plant cells.

cell wall: a tough layer outside the cell membrane; found in the cells of plants, fungi and bacteria.

cellulose: a carbohydrate that forms long fibres, and makes up the cell walls of plants.

central nervous system (CNS): the brain and spinal cord.

chlorophyll: a green pigment (coloured substance) that absorbs energy from light; the energy is used to combine carbon dioxide with water to make glucose.

chromosome: a length of DNA, found in the nucleus of a cell; it contains genetic information in the form of many different genes.

circulatory system: a system of blood vessels with a pump and valves to ensure one-way flow of blood.

clone: an identical copy of something.

community: all of the populations of all the different species in an ecosystem.

complementary: with a perfect mirror-image shape.

compound: a substance formed by the chemical combination of two or more elements in fixed proportions

concentration gradient: an imaginary 'slope' from a high concentration to a low concentration.

continuous variation: variation in which there is a continuous range of phenotypes between two extremes.

cuticle: a thin layer of wax that covers the upper surface of a leaf.

cytoplasm: the jelly-like material that fills a cell.

decomposer: an organism that gets its energy from dead or waste organic matter.

deoxygenated blood: blood containing only a little oxygen.

dependent variable: the variable that you measure as you collect your results.

diet: the food eaten in one day.

diffusion: the net movement of particles from a region of their higher concentration to a region of their lower concentration (i.e. down a concentration gradient), as a result of their random movement.

digestion: the breakdown of food.

diploid: having two complete sets of chromosomes.

discontinuous variation: variation in which there are distinct categories of phenotype, with no intermediates.

DNA: a molecule that contains genetic information, in the form of genes, that controls the proteins that are made in the cell.

dominant allele: an allele that is expressed if it is present (e.g. **G**).

double circulatory system: a system in which blood passes through the heart twice on one complete circuit of the body.

duodenum: the first part of the small intestine, into which the pancreatic duct and bile duct empty fluids.

ecosystem: a unit containing all of the organisms in a community and their environment, interacting together.

emulsion: a liquid containing two substances that do not fully mix; one of them forms tiny droplets dispersed throughout the other.

endangered species: species that are found in very low numbers, which means that they are at risk of extinction.

endocrine glands: glands that secrete hormones.

enzyme–substrate complex: the short-lived structure formed as the substrate binds temporarily to the active site of an enzyme.

enzymes: proteins that are involved in all metabolic reactions, where they function as biological catalysts.

excretion: the removal of waste products of metabolism and substances in excess of requirements.

extinction: the process that leads to the complete absence of a species.

fats: lipids that are solid at room temperature.

fertilisation: the fusion of the nuclei of two gametes.

flaccid: a description of a plant cell that is soft

flagellum (plural flagella): a long, whip-like 'tail' structure found on sperm cells, used for swimming.

food chain: a diagram showing the transfer of energy from one organism to the next, beginning with a producer.

food web: a network of interconnected food chains.

fossil fuel: a non-renewable substance that can be burnt to release energy.

fully permeable: allows all molecules and ions to pass through it.

gall bladder: a small organ that stores bile, before the bile is released into the duodenum.

gamete: a sex cell; a cell with half the normal number of chromosomes, whose nucleus fuses with the nucleus of another gamete during sexual reproduction.

gas exchange: the diffusion of oxygen and carbon dioxide into and out of an organism's body.

gas exchange surface: a part of the body where gas exchange between the body and the environment takes place.

gene: a length of DNA that codes for one protein.

genetic diagram: a standard way of showing all the steps in making predictions about the probable genotypes and phenotypes of the offspring from two parents.

genotype: the genetic makeup of an organism in terms of the alleles present (e.g. **GG**).

glucose: a sugar that is used in respiration to release energy.

glycogen: a carbohydrate that is used as an energy store in animal cells.

growth: a permanent increase in size and dry mass.

habitat: the place where an organism lives.

haemoglobin: a red pigment found in red blood cells, which can combine reversibly with oxygen; it is a protein.

haploid: having only a single set of chromosomes.

heterozygous: having two different alleles of a particular gene (e.g. **Gg**).

high water potential: an area where there are a lot of water molecules – a dilute solution.

HIV/AIDS: an infectious disease caused by the viral pathogen human immunodeficiency virus (HIV), which is transmitted through the sexual and blood-to-blood contact routes and can cause weakening of the immune system, leaving patients susceptible to other diseases.

homozygous: having two identical alleles of a particular gene (e.g. **GG** or **gg**).

hormones: chemicals that are produced by a gland and carried in the blood, which alter the activities of their specific target organs.

immune response: the reaction of the body to the presence of an antigen; it involves the production of antibodies.

independent variable: the variable that you change in an experiment.

insecticide: a chemical that kills insects.

insulin: a hormone secreted by the pancreas, which decreases blood glucose concentration.

iodine solution: a solution of iodine in potassium iodide; it is orange-brown, and turns blue-black when mixed with starch.

lipids: substances containing carbon, hydrogen and oxygen; they are insoluble in water and are used as energy stores in organisms.

low water potential: an area where there are not many water molecules – a concentrated solution.

magnification: how many times larger an image is than the actual object.

meiosis: division of a diploid nucleus, resulting in four genetically different haploid nuclei; this is sometimes called a reduction division.

memory cells: long-lived cells produced by the division of lymphocytes that have contacted their antigen; memory cells are able to respond quickly to subsequent contact with the same antigen.

metabolic reactions: chemical reactions that take place in living organisms.

mitochondrion: a small structure in a cell, where aerobic respiration releases energy from glucose.

mitosis: division of a cell nucleus, resulting in two genetically identical nuclei (that is, with the same number and kinds of chromosomes as the parent nucleus).

motor neurone: a neurone that transmits electrical impulses from the central nervous system to an effector.

movement: an action by an organism or part of an organism causing a change of position or place.

nectar: a sweet liquid secreted by many insect-pollinated flowers, to attract their pollinators.

negative feedback: a mechanism that detects a move away from the set point, and brings about actions that take the value back towards the set point.

nerve impulse: an electrical signal that passes rapidly along an axon.

net movement: overall or average movement.

neurone: a cell that is specialised for conducting electrical impulses rapidly.

nucleus: a structure containing DNA in the form of chromosomes.

nutrition: the taking in of materials for energy, growth and development.

oils: lipids that are liquid at room temperature.

optimum: best; for example, the optimum temperature of an enzyme is the temperature at which its activity is greatest.

organism: a living thing.

osmosis: the diffusion of water molecules through a partially permeable membrane.

osmosis: (in terms of water potential) the net movement of water molecules from a region of higher water potential (dilute solution) to a region of lower water potential (concentrated solution) through a partially permeable membrane.

oxygenated blood: blood containing a lot of oxygen.

palisade mesophyll: the layer of cells immediately beneath the upper epidermis, where most photosynthesis happens.

pancreas: a creamy-white organ lying close to the stomach, which secretes pancreatic juice; it also secretes the hormones insulin and glucagon, which are involved in the control of blood glucose concentration.

partially permeable: allows some molecules and ions to pass through, but not others.

partially permeable membrane: a membrane (very thin layer) that lets some particles move through it, but prevents others passing through.

particles: (in this context) the smallest pieces of which a substance is made; particles can be molecules, atoms or ions.

pathogens: microorganisms that cause disease.

peripheral nervous system (PNS): the nerves outside the brain and spinal cord.

petals: coloured structures that attract insects or birds to a flower.

phenotype: the observable features of an organism.

phloem: a plant tissue that transports substances made by the plant, such as sucrose and amino acids.

photosynthesis: the process by which plants synthesise carbohydrates from raw materials using energy from light.

plasma: the liquid part of blood.

plasmolysed: a description of a cell in which the cell membrane has torn away from the cell wall.

platelets: tiny cell fragments present in blood, which help with clotting.

pollen grains: small structures which contain the male gametes of a flower.

pollination: the transfer of pollen grains from the male part of the plant (anther of stamen) to the female part of the plant (stigma).

product: the new substance formed by a chemical reaction.

proteins: substances whose molecules are made of many amino acids linked together; each different protein has a different sequence of amino acids.

pulmonary artery: the artery that carries deoxygenated blood from the right ventricle to the lungs.

pulmonary veins: the veins that carry oxygenated blood from the lungs to the left atrium of the heart.

range: the lowest to the highest value.

receptors: cells or groups of cells that detect stimuli.

recessive allele: an allele that is only expressed when there is no dominant allele of the gene present (e.g. **g**).

red blood cells: biconcave blood cells with no nucleus, which transport oxygen.

reducing sugars: sugars such as glucose, which turn Benedict's solution orange-red when heated together.

reflex action: a rapid, automatic response to a stimulus, which does not involve conscious thought.

reflex arc: a series of neurones (sensory, relay and motor) that transmit electrical impulses from a receptor to an effector.

relay neurone: a neurone that transmits electrical impulses within the central nervous system.

reproduction: the processes that make more of the same kind of organism.

respiration: the chemical reactions in cells that break down nutrient molecules and release energy for metabolism.

ribosomes: very small structures in a cell that use information in DNA to make protein molecules.

salivary glands: groups of cells close to the mouth, which secrete saliva into the salivary ducts.

selection pressure: something in the environment that affects the chance that individuals with different features will survive and reproduce.

selective breeding: choosing particular organisms with desired characteristics to breed together, and continuing this over many generations.

sensitivity: the ability to detect and respond to changes in the internal or external environment.

sensory neurone: a neurone that transmits electrical impulses from a receptor to the central nervous system.

set point: the normal value, or range of values, for a particular parameter – for example, the normal range of blood glucose concentration, or the normal body temperature.

sexual reproduction: a process involving the fusion of two gametes to form a zygote and the production of offspring that are genetically different from each other.

single circulatory system: a system in which blood passes through the heart only once on one complete circuit of the body.

sink: part of a plant to which sucrose or amino acids are being transported, and where they are used or stored.

small intestine: a long, narrow part of the alimentary canal, consisting of the duodenum and ileum.

source: part of a plant that releases sucrose or amino acids, to be transported to other parts.

specificity: (of enzymes) only able to act on a particular (specific) substrate.

spongy mesophyll: the layer of cells immediately beneath the palisade mesophyll, where some photosynthesis happens; this tissue contains a lot of air spaces between the cells.

starch: a carbohydrate that is used as an energy store in plant cells.

stigma: the part of a flower that receives pollen.

stimuli: changes in the environment that can be detected by organisms.

stomach: a wide part of the alimentary canal, in which food can be stored for a while, and where the digestion of protein begins.

stomata (singular: stoma): openings in the surface of a leaf, most commonly in the lower surface; they are surrounded by pairs of guard cells, which control whether the stomata are open or closed.

substrate: the substance that an enzyme acts upon.

sucrose: a sugar whose molecules are made of glucose and another similar molecule (fructose) linked together.

sugars: carbohydrates that have relatively small molecules; they are soluble in water and they taste sweet.

target organs: organs whose activity is altered by a hormone.

transmissible disease: a disease that can be passed from one host to another; transmissible diseases are caused by pathogens.

trophic level: the position of an organism in a food chain, food web or ecological pyramid.

turgid: a description of a plant cell that is tight and firm.

turgor pressure: the pressure of the water pushing outwards on a plant cell wall.

type 1 diabetes: a condition in which insufficient insulin is secreted by the pancreas, so that blood glucose concentration is not controlled.

vaccine: a harmless preparation of dead or inactivated pathogens that is injected into the body to induce an immune response.

vacuole: a fluid-filled space inside a cell, separated from the cytoplasm by a membrane.

valves: structures that allow a liquid to flow in one direction only.

vena cava: the large vein that brings deoxygenated blood to the right atrium.

ventricles: the thick-walled chambers at the base of the heart, which pump out blood.

water potential gradient: a difference in water potential between two areas.

white blood cells: blood cells with a nucleus, which help to defend against pathogens.

xylem: a plant tissue that transports water and mineral ions and helps to support the plant.

zygote: a cell that is formed by the fusion of two gametes.

> Acknowledgements

The authors and publishers acknowledge the following sources of copyright material and are grateful for the permissions granted. While every effort has been made, it has not always been possible to identify the sources of all the material used, or to trace all copyright holders. If any omissions are brought to our notice, we will be happy to include the appropriate acknowledgements on reprinting.

Thanks to the following for permission to reproduce images:

Cover Sebastien GABORIT/GI; *Inside* Figure 1.3 Eleanor Jones; Figure 7.3 Dr Keith Wheeler/ Science Photo Library